OPTIONS

TRADING

*Tips and Tricks to Learn all about Options
Trading and upscale your Income*

ERIC WILLIAMS

TABLE OF CONTENTS

Introduction

The internet has opened the door to financial instruments and given us the chance to make money online. Before the internet, you will have to go through banks and other financial institutions to invest and make money from these markets. Also, it has become faster to trade with the internet, and we are now open to much information before that can help us trade these markets effectively.

One of the ways we can make money in the financial market is through trading options. This book will enlighten you about this market, the best strategies to employ, and some useful tips and tricks that will help you make money online. Options are traded as derivatives of other financial instruments such as shares, commodities, EFT, and stocks. For example, we can trade the derivatives of stocks while not actually owning the shares of the company.

We do not need to buy shares in Apple or Facebook to trade and make money as a derivative in the options market. We are predicting where the assets will move over a period of time, and that is the simplest explanation to understand how options work.

You may be wondering what secrets we are going to reveal in this book?

To be honest, there are no secrets to reveal in this book, but the knowledge that you will need to trade the market successfully. With the application of this knowledge, you are bound to improve your trading skills and make yourself some money in this business.

We have come to understand that one of the reasons people fail in the financial market is the lack of knowledge and the application of this knowledge. The understanding of how these instruments move is important, and then there is a need to understand the physiology involved to become a successful trader.

This book will also tell us why we should select options trading from other instruments to make money, such as Forex trading, shares, binary, and other financial instruments online. It does not matter if you are fully employed or unemployed; you can make money through options trading.

With the help of this book in building an understanding of options trading, beginners can be able to fully understand and comprehend how it differs from other forms of online trading. The eBook is not only suitable for the newbie but can also help advanced traders as a refresher course and providing strategies that can help them make money.

We are going to discuss some of the best strategies that will help us achieve your aim of making money. One of the reasons we have realized people lose money trading online is the strategy or lack of it they use. Here, you are going to learn well-researched strategies that will increase your chances of making profits with your trades. Another reason for losing money is because they are also not prepared mentally to trade options, so they fail even with a good strategy. And at the end of the book, you will understand the importance of psychological trading and how it will impact a trader's success in the market.

With some physiological tips and tricks, you can make a steady income from the trading of options. Just read the book with an open mindset and follow the step by step instructions in this book and become financially stable with options trading.

Chapter 1

What is Options Trading?

Now we are going to get to the business, but first, we are going to explain what options trading entails. The term can be confusing, and most people have not really got the grasp of options trading other than the way they have done with Forex, shares, and bet on the market.

Shares involve buying part of a company, and making money while the share price increases, and from a dividend of the shares. It is kind of straightforward, you may think, but it involves lots of fundamental and technical study of the market to make a steady income. There are many uncertainties and factors that control the market and make it difficult. So making money from shares can be difficult, and many people prefer to leave it for the experts.

Another way of making money online is Forex trading which involves buying and selling of one currency over another currency. Forex has become really common with so many Forex brokers springing up to compete for millions of traders that want to trade Forex. The Forex market controls billions of dollars daily, and it can go either way, so traders use fundamental and technical analysis to predict which currency will be volatile and which direction the particular currency will move over the other currency.

With Forex trading, you are trading two pairs as you expect one pair to go up or go down over the other. So, you can see that trading Forex is also direct and easy to understand, but it can be difficult to make a steady income from this market. The most traded currency pairs are the

EUR/USD, and when you go bearish, it indicates that you will gain when the pair falls while with a bullish market, the Euro gains as the pair go up, and you make money buying the pair.

Forex is easy to understand, and you can start trading as soon as possible because it is easy to learn. You can use the fundamental or technical analysis or a combination of both analyses.

Options trading is a different ballgame with lots of terms you have to understand to be able to know what is happening in the market. Without grasping these terms, you cannot trade successfully because you will be lost about events taking place on the platform. So the first step is to understand the different terms, what you will be trading, and how to trade these derivatives.

But in a real sense, options trading is more flexible and provides you with a more profitable probability than trading shares or Forex. With the latter, you will need a considerable amount of capital and deep knowledge of how to trade before you can succeed.

The amount of investment needs to start the business makes it difficult for people to trade Forex or shares. For example, buying shares at the present price will require you to invest huge amounts of money to buy more shares to stand a chance of making a considerable profit.

Options trading involves the buying or selling of contracts at a stipulated amount for a period of time. The investment portfolio for options trading may include shares, ETFs, and mutual funds. However, the contract will stipulate when you want to make and collect your profit when it falls or rises. It is as simple as that; you can make a profit if it moves up or loses when it goes down.

Unlike shares and trading ETFs, there is more flexibility in investing in this kind of trade. You can bet on the directions of any of the markets without having access to the shares of the company. You can invest in top shares of companies even if you do not have the money to invest in such companies. For example, the shares of Apple may not readily be available for you to buy, or the price may be so high that you cannot afford a reasonable amount of the shares that could amount to a reasonable profit. But with options trading and knowledge of how the shares will move in the market, you can bet that the shares will move either up or down for a certain period of time.

We can now define option trading as a contract, buying, or selling a certain amount of shares of a company or entity that will expire at a certain period of time. It is a derivative of other financial instruments as the market moves, and traders predict the moves of the market. With options trading, you are not buying the shares or the stocks directly but leveraging on the movements of these assets with options provided by the brokers.

Options trading does give you the opportunity to trade many financial markets such as shares, mutual funds, and ETFs, which will not be accessible to you on other forms of the financial market. Imagine the opportunity that stands before you when you have access to various markets to make money, and all you have to do is find out if the market is going up, down, or it will remain stagnant.

In options trading, it is so simple that you only have to find out which three directions the market will move. The market will either move in the following direction:

1. It will go up

2. It will go down

3. Or it will remain stagnant.

Very easy, right? Nothing is that easy as it may seem, for the real deal is trading the market live.

It may be easy if you have experience trading other markets such as Forex and shares, where it is not difficult to analyze what direction the market will move to make money.

When you buy a contract in options trading, you are permitted but not limited to do the following with the contract.

1. Make a transaction of stock at the strike price of the market, which you may hold for a certain period of time. Everything concerning that contract, including the amount of time to hold the contract, will be agreed to before the execution of the contract.

2. You have the option to sell the contract to another investor during the period that the contract is valid.

3. Allow the contract to run its course and be free from my obligation to the contract.

4. You can also sell the contract if you feel that it will end up as a loss or you want to take your profit before the time expires.

I am sure it is getting interesting now; I guess most of you, especially the newbies, have never viewed options trading in this way.

Any kind of trader or investor can invest in options trading, from the short-term trader to the long-term trader and even those looking for ways to make fast cash.

But I would strongly recommend that if you are getting into options trading to find a time frame, you can manage with your style of trading. Choose the timeframe you will be available to trade in when you need to and one that you feel comfortable with while trading.

Why You Should Trade Option

Do you think options trading is a new form of financial instrument? Then you must be mistaken, for they have been around for over 40 years. However, they have not been as popular as shares and bond trading mainly because of the many misconceptions associated with them.

For one, it is not easy to understand options like all other forms on the financial market, and there have not been many positive reviews about options trading. One of such reasons is the lack of experience from brokers as well as traders who have managed to make huge losses on the platforms.

Another is the misunderstanding that options trading is much more difficult, although I would agree that the terms are not easy to understand. But once you get the knack of it, it grows on you, and you can make huge money from options.

At this stage, we are going to share the advantages options trading hold over other forms of trading. I believe when you are done with analyzing these advantages, your interest in option trading will spike up, and you will be ready to go to the next stage.

1. Cost Efficiency

Buying shares of a company will require substantial investment. However, obtaining the same position on options trading will require less investment and huge savings in return. Supposing, you believe that shares in Apple will be rising very soon and want to buy shares to gain from this anticipated surge in the share price. A share of Apple costs say $100, for example, and you wish to buy 100 shares, which will equate to you spending $100 000 on your investment.

Once the share goes up, you will be expecting a huge return, but the investment is quite substantial in the beginning. How many people can afford to invest that much money in shares? Also, it is quite a risk, knowing that nothing is certain when investing in the financial markets. On the other hand, shares may not be available to buy on the market since they are not for public sale.

With options trading, you will be risking less money to leverage the anticipated move-in share prices. When you opt for options trading, you will be buying the contract at a certain price, known as "strike price," and can expect to make some percentage of the profit at the stipulated time the contract will expire.

Let's say the strike price of the contract is $10 for 100 shares on the Apple stock. You will now pay $1000 for the contract to make a profit when the price goes up after the contract expires according to your calculation.

You have saved quite a huge amount of money, aiming for the same result on the price of Apple shares rising. You will save $90 000 and risk just $1000. And it is affordable for those who cannot make a huge investment to buy a considerable amount of shares in the company to make a substantial profit.

So one of the advantages is the cost-effective nature of investing in the financial market with options trading, and you can take advantage of this market, starting with a relatively small investment.

2. Options are Dependable and Less Risky

Trading financial instruments are risky, but in our dealings, we like to reduce the risk to the minimal. You might lose money on any trade you make on financial instruments, but the limit we place on the money we intend to loss will determine the risk we are taking with that transaction.

In this case, options are known to be less risky than stock or trading equity. With trading on some of these popular platforms, you can place a stop loss on your trade, to take account of the potential loss of a percentage of your capital. Using stop loss is advisable to reduce the risk of losing your capital in the market.

With a stop loss, you can calculate the amount of money you will likely lose in the trade if it goes against your prediction. For example, you can place a stop loss to a loss of $100 when the market hits a particular point to cut off your losses. The profit may be equal to the stop or higher than the stop depending on your target.

The purpose of using this stop loss is to minimize loss and prevent the liquidation of your account for one trade gone wrong. If the stock continues going against the direction you intend, then you can count your $100 loss and look for another trade.

It is advisable to limit your stop loss to 10 or 20% of your capital. However, the gap in stock trading can cause you to lose beyond the limit you set for the trade. The stop loss does not respect gaps when the market opens, and this is the disadvantage of trading stocks and equity.

Stocks and equity are not open 24 hours a day, so when the market closes, high impact news can affect the market before it opens. The market may react to the news negatively and cause the market to open way beyond your stop loss.

Because the market cannot react when closed, it may open way beyond your stop loss and may cause a huge amount of deficit. Your loss may have exceeded the stop loss of $100, which will make you lose more than you intended in the trade. It may wipe out your capital if the news impact affects the market to a great extent.

The reverse will be the case with options trading, which is more flexible and opens 24 hours a day, seven days a week. You have access to the platform to react to the news that may be affecting your positions immediately you get the news that may affect the market at any time of the day.

3. Options offer higher percentage returns

With options, you can earn more by spending less, which offers a higher percentage of returns than stock. Investing $50 in stock may earn you 10% returns in a move that may earn you over 80 % returns when trading options, and you can invest as little as $6 in that move.

There is a way that the percentage return is calculated in an option that you can earn up to 80% when the market moves in the right direction with a minimal investment.

4. The option is open for all investors.

Option trading is more flexible than stocks or equity, and you do not require a huge investment to gain in the market. Anyone can trade options, for you do not need to learn complicated techniques or stay online to make profit trading options.

A considerable amount of money is needed to invest in a stock, buying substantial shares that will yield your income. With options trading, you may not need to invest huge capital to make a reasonable profit.

With a small amount of money, you can make huge returns with options trading. So it opens the door for small as well as large-scale investors to make money with this instrument.

With $50, your returns on shares maybe just 10%, but the same investment in option reading might yield you 80%.

5. Options offer flexible and strategic alternative trading

Trading stock is very much one-directional, as you either trade high or low, but option offers flexible options for trading. With stock, your trade is based mainly on the volatility of the market to move up or down in big moves. Trading stagnant or low volume markets is a huge risk with shares and equity.

Options offer you a wide range of trading options and alternatives as you can trade the market in different ways. You can trade up, down or sideways when the market is fluctuating. You can trade the market when it is low in volume and when stagnant. Offering you different ways of making money, options are easier to read than shares with its complex nature of finding a suitable entry point and target.

With stock trading, some brokers may place restrictions on your activities on the platform that include charges on each trade, restrictions on shorting shares, and other restrictions and limits. But option trading offers you more flexible options for trading. You can trade shares of stocks going up or down; you can trade sideways movements, you can also trade volatility such as the time the volatility will last and its impact.

So the flexibility of options trading makes it possible to hit more trades and make money. Stocks and shares are limited in their approach, and you may be forced to choose a position when the options are not much.

In a nutshell, we can see that options trading has more advantages than stock or shares with its flexibility and options available to trade various options. Now, you have to dedicate time to learn how to trade options, and with so many online brokers available, you now have access from anywhere to trade the options market.

Although it is one of the most complicated financial instruments, it offers variable options to make money. And with online access to brokers, you have no excuse for not being part of the most profitable form of the financial market.

Challenges You Face with Option Trading

After reviewing the advantages of options trading right to you getting to know the limitations you will face with trading options, newbies will find it difficult to get the hang of options trading and without following the right instructions, may acquire some losses.

Hedge funds operators and speculators make use of this effective tool to analyze the market. Individuals trading options, however, should pay more attention to the magnitude of the intended move so as not to lose money in their trade.

Everything that has an advantage does have its limitation, and this is the case with options trading. We are going to list out some of the limitations you will face in options trading as a guide to make your trading profitable. The knowledge of these limitations is not to discourage you in trading options but to guide you on how to trade options correctly. You will avoid those pitfalls that inexperienced traders will fall prey to in the process of learning these limitations.

• Options have an expiry date

Options as a trading tool expire, and you cannot hold the options more than the stipulated time on the contract, unlike shares that you can hold for a long time until you decide to sell off the stocks. You can also transfer these shares to another person or group of persons; you can transfer them as well to your children. An option is not transferable, and you will have to cash out on your profit or loss after the contract expires.

Options are not suitable for long-term investors, or those that want to own part of a company. They are mostly suitable for hedging on shares and to make quick profits.

Nevertheless, this does not make it a good investment for traders who are looking to make passive or regular incomes on financial securities.

• Possibility of loss of all investment

Trading shares, you can sell the shares whenever you want to, especially when the shares are not performing as you would have expected. In so doing, you may be able to recuperate some of the money you invested even if the shares fall below the price you bought them for earlier.

With options, you run the risk of losing everything you invested in the trade once it goes against you. When the contract expires, and it does not fulfill the option you desire, you will lose all you invested in that trade at the time the contract expires. So unless you are very sure that the trade will go in the direction you speculate, you stand a higher chance of losing all your investment in that trade.

• The danger of leverage

The leverage you enjoy with options trading also has its danger to your trading account. With options trading, you can make more money from as little investment as you wish to place on the trade. You can increase your earnings more than 50% of your investment in one trade based on the leverage you enjoy with options.

Leverage can become dangerous because it may get you to overtrade since you may feel that you are investing a small amount to gain a higher percentage of money. The options market is a speculative market with high risk, and trading too much exposes your account to high drawdown.

● The volatility of the market

The options price is a derivative of the share prices, but share prices do not move as fast as options. The volatility of options is high, and it may make huge moves in a single day, and the intended position can change very fast.

With shares, your position may not change drastically unless there is some kind of bad news that may drive the range of change very high. When the range of change is very high, it may take some time for the market price to return to the point where it may favor you.

But on the other hand, options trading offers you the opportunity to trade other markets when one does not have high volatility.

It is highly speculative

Shares and some other forms of the financial market are traded with technical and fundamental knowledge of the market. You can draw out some specific strategies to trade these financial instruments and develop a pattern over time. However, options trading is highly speculative, although we can still develop some trading patterns to make us consistent in our own trading pattern.

You should understand that none of these trading instruments can give you 100% trade success, but the development of methods helps to increase the rate of success.

However, the speculative rate of this market makes you frequently trade, which increases your chances of losing in the market. The nature of the market makes it easier for traders to find opportunities in the market, which increases the chance of losing.

The more you find yourself trading, the more risk you take on in the market. And options trading provides you with several opportunities to trade on the platform.

● **Options can be confusing**
One of the reasons you find fewer people trading options is that it is confusing and not like other financial instruments. It is not as direct as shares or stocks and will require time to understand the terminologies and other terms involved in an options trade.

When trading options, you do not intend to hit a target or hold the asset indefinitely until you want to sell it and take your profit. It is a time decay instrument, and it is hard to predict the price of an asset at a particular time. This is the reason we say that this investment is highly speculative and you will require a deep knowledge of the market to succeed and predict the moves correctly

As we have highlighted the advantages and limitations of options trading, I believe that we have a wider understanding of what we expect in this market. I am sure whatever your purpose of trading options: for hedging of funds or for making money as an extra income or consistent income, you know what you will be against by now.

While still in the early stage of the process of being successful in options trading, we still need to understand some of the terms and how we can trade options successfully. As we progress with this book, the preceding chapters will dwell more on how to trade options and some of the useful methods we will use in trading options

By the time you have finished reading this book, you will not only understand what options trading is about, but you should also be trading options successfully.

It is a step-by-step process, and I will encourage you to go through all the steps and guides in this book. Let it be your main resource in becoming a successful trader.

Chapter 2

How to Trade Options

Now, we will be getting into the business of how to trade options. In this chapter, we are going to show you how to start trading Forex from scratch, what you will need to start, and all the process of creating your trading account, including the suitable brokers to use.

With options trading, you are not buying directly into the shares of the company, but rather, you are speculating the direction the shares will go at a stipulated time.

With options trading, you are buying 100 shares of the company at a strike price, speculating if the shares will go up, down, or remain sideways.

The first process involved in options trading is opening an account that will require you to submit the necessary information to the selected broker. Selecting the perfect broker is another process in opening an account, but we are going to deal with that one later.

Opening an Option Trading Account

You will need to provide certain personal information for the broker to access your ability to trade options. We understand the complexity of trading options, and the broker wants to ensure that you are ready to take the risk in the market. They will have to analyze you based on the questions that you will answer on their platform.

The analysis will involve knowing how prepared you are in trading options based on your knowledge of the market and the amount of capital you are willing to invest in. To trade options, you will need a considerable amount of capital, although not as substantial as you will need to buy shares or stocks

In filling out forms provided by the broker before opening an account, you will need to provide the following information:

- **Personal information**

  You will fill out your personal information containing your name, date of birth, nationality, and other personal data required by the broker. This is required to authenticate the person that wants to open the account, which will be verified with some form of identification as required.

- **Investment objective**

  The broker may like to know the purpose of opening the account, your investment objectives, and how you intend to trade using the account. The questions in this section will determine if you are trading for income, to grow your resources, preserve capital, or for speculative purposes.

- **Trading experience**

  The next requirement will have you display your trading experience if you have traded any financial instruments such as stocks or shares. And your experience, which is how many years you have been trading any of these instruments. Your knowledge and experience are needed by the broker to understand the kind of investor coming to the platform.

- **Your financial record**

  Your financial record is required at this stage, and this will include your income, net worth, and your employment information. You will have to indicate if you are unemployed, self-employed, or employed, and your yearly income at this session.

- **Indicate the type of option**

  Further information will require the type of option you want to trade, and you will be asked this by the broker.

  All of this information will be required by the broker to create an account on the platform and start trading options. The format of gathering personal information may differ from one broker to another, but these are the general information items that will be needed to be completed.

  The broker will place you on a class according to your trading experience and your financial record. This classification will help you in trading, as they will place you in a particular class providing the required support for your levels of trading.

  The broker usually provides support in terms of trading materials, leverages, and bonuses that will help you become successful. When you provide them with the right information, this will determine the level of support they will provide to you to enable you to trade conveniently on the platform. Thus, it's important, to be honest.

Factors to Consider in Choosing an Option Broker

A broker is like the middleman, the platform you will go through to execute your trade. They provide you with all the available options, their market values, and a commission fee for each trade.

The broker brings the market to you, where you execute your trade, and they register the trade for you. There are so many brokers out there that can offer you these services. But choosing the right one is vital for your trading.

Choosing the right broker can make a difference in trading options successfully. Take your time in choosing the right broker amongst the numerous you will find online, especially choosing one that suits your style and personality.

Although the decision to choose a broker can be reversed, you will have wasted time, resources, and money with an unfavorable broker. Some people have given up on options and other financial instruments because of the services of their broker.

So making the right choice at the beginning is important if you want to make income from this business.

What are we going to consider when choosing a broker? How are we going to know if a broker will be right for us?

It is unfortunate that some people pick the first broker that they come across online. Or select the oldest broker, thinking that being in the business for a long time makes them better than others.

Research about different brokers and select the one that suits you as a trader. Brokers go through changes with the latest technology and innovation. The new ones may be better with advanced technology and services than the older ones if they fail to upgrade their services.

So proper research will guide you as to what is happening in these brokerage firms and how it will affect your trading.

Selecting a broker is part of the trading, and it is right that you do that yourself. We are going to discuss some of the factors that will guide you in choosing the right broker for your options trading.

Commission and Fee of the Broker

In options trading, we are dealing with money, and we have to put into consideration how much you will be spending. Each broker has its commission; you will pay for trades, and they also have some additional fees you will pay for their services.

These charges will seem minimal, but when you sum it up over time, it will add up to a substantial amount. For each trade you make regardless of whether you are buying or selling, you will have to pay a commission. The broker will take this commission for executing the trade. It is an amount you pay for the services they are offering to you.

Is there anything wrong with paying these commissions?

Absolutely not, every broker charges a commission, and it is one way they make their money. However, you should make sure that the charges are not higher than others may offer. It is unfortunate that most traders do not take these charges into consideration and may end up paying more than they would otherwise have been paying.

Don't get it wrong, feeling that the amount is minimal. For if your broker charges $2 per trade, you would have spent 2 x 50 = $100 for 50 trades.

Now let's look at another broker offering $1 per trade you make. That will be 1 x 50 = $50 for 50 trades.

Using the latter broker, you will be saving $50 for every 50 trades you will make on the platform. Imagine those traders that make more trades with the example we have mentioned. They will be saving a considerable amount of money in the long run.

So always find out the commission you will be paying for each trade, for it will save you lots of money. If you find out that your broker is overcharging you when compared to other brokers, you can easily switch. In the long run, you will be making more money with a broker that charges less commission for trading.

Before choosing a broker, you can check out the reviews from customers. You will learn certain things, especially their commissions on trades.

On the other hand, brokers may have additional fees you may be obliged to pay for the services rendered. Brokers may ask you to pay for a wide range of services, which may include payment for deposit and withdrawals, monthly or yearly fees, maintenance fees, and charges for offering certain services or for some particular transaction you may make. These fees may add up to a considerable amount of money, so it's important that you take them into consideration.

We must get something straight; these charges can also be of huge benefit to your trading. Some of these charges may invoke offering you expert support that will help your trading. They may also be offering services such as providing current news or offering you trade advisory services to help you make money.

In such instances, some traders may be willing to pay for those services to help traders make good decisions on the market. Newbies can use these services to help them gain more knowledge in the earlier part of their trading experience. Brokers may also offer you services that will help you interact with traders. You can copy trades and make profits; however, these services come at a premium price. Not everyone will have the money to spend on such services, but it may be worth it, especially for inexperienced traders.

If you do not have the money to pay for these services, you can always opt for discount brokers. The discount brokers have reduced the cost of operating a trader's account and usually offer services at the reduced commission for your transactions, while the full option brokers offer you the full services that include assistance from the broker and other experienced brokers.

In trying to cut costs and increase the propensity of making more profit, a cheap broker is not a necessity. A broker offering low charges in commission and services may not end up being the best broker for you. It is just one of the factors you have to consider in choosing a broker.

One piece of advice I would give to anyone entering the options market is to go for a full-service broker. They may be more expensive with their additional services but may be worth it at the end of the day.

As a newbie, you will get the much-needed help and assistance to grow in the business. View the money you will spend on the services as an investment in learning how to trade successfully.

After a while, when you have gained the necessary knowledge, you can switch the broker. Use the brokers that provide additional support to enhance your trading skills and later switch to a discount broker.

Before you sign up for a broker, know about their structures and commission payments. Check out their charges and make sure you understand what the companies are offering and the charges you may pay using the broker so you do not end up getting caught with charges that you may not want to pay for using the broker.

Consider your own trading skills and the type of trading you carry out to ensure that you do not lose much with charges. An understanding of all the commissions and fees will help you plan your trade and manage your investments.

Speed of Execution of Order and the Quality of Execution

When you place an order, you are sure at that moment that the trade will move from that price to the direction you are anticipating. So you want that order executed as fast as possible to maximize your profit and not to miss out on the opportunity.

The speed of execution is another important factor to consider when choosing a broker. The speed will go a long way toward determining your success at trading options. Traders have been left frustrated with the creeping nature of their chosen platforms. A good broker will execute your order as fast as possible to get you in the right direction of the trade.

Markets move very fast, especially during a period of high volatility and high impact news. So the fast execution of the contract is important if you want to take due advantage of such big moves.

Why is the speed of execution different from one platform to the other?

The answer lies in the platform of the broker and their ability to respond to execution. Some brokers fail to execute transactions fast because of their slow nature to respond. They may not have upgraded to much better technology software for their platform. Using the latest platform to ensure speed of execution is one of the criteria of choosing the broker to use.

Check the platform of the broker and make sure they use an updated platform, so you do not get ripped off by a slow platform. If you experience a slow pace in opening pages on their site, take this as a warning sign when using these platforms. Read customer reviews about the broker to check what people write about their speed of execution and response time of the platform.

I have used several brokers during my years of trading. As a newbie, I did not pay attention to such issues as the speed of execution. Using a particular broker, I lost many opportunities for entering the market because of the slow platform of the broker. It failed to put me in the market at the time I placed the trade and thus moved out of the price I intended to enter before the broker placed my trade.

One other drawback of these slow speeds in the execution of orders is the psychological effect. You become disoriented when you miss an opportunity to enter a trade, and this might lead to trading against your plan. Also, imagine taking longer for your platform to sign in and execute a trade. On such occasions, before you sign in to your account, you may have lost the opportunity to enter a profitable trade. These are some of the losses you may experience using a broker that does not respond fast.

I changed my broker after much research on the best broker with good speed. And my trading experience improved considerably, with faster execution and ability to make a profit when you enter at the right time.

Do not be too worried about it as in the course of this book; we will provide you with some of the best brokers for newbie and experienced traders.

Brokers with User-Friendly Platform

Imagine you have spent time learning how to trade options, only to end up with a difficult platform. Some brokers have complicated platforms that require the trader to spend some time learning how to use the platform. The platforms may also be so complicated that it will take time to execute the trade.

So check the ease of using the platform before signing up for the platform. A user-friendly platform should have all the required tools easily accessible on the platform. You do not want to be reading the chart and have to go to another page to buy or sell on the platform. This is a waste of time as we need an easy to use platform where you can easily do your transaction and read your charts from the same place.

Using a platform that is complicated will waste time in finding charts, executing trades, and managing trades on the platform.

In my first year of trading, I used several trading platforms, and with one, you had to spend more time executing your trade than when using another platform. So I do not have to explain to you what my next step was. I had to move away from the one with the slow pace of execution and processing. Some platforms look so dull and may not be inspiring.

Most of the platforms use a common trading system that traders are familiar with, so stick to what is common in other platforms. So when you are reading reviews during the research on a potentially suitable broker, ensure that you make a point of choosing a user-friendly platform.

Security of the Broker

Being able to trade online is an advantage we have since the Internet age is now the best way forward. However, this is also affected by the high rate of online hacking we have seen in recent times. We have heard of top financial institutions being hacked of financial reports at the risk of being exposed. This is the major threat we have with selecting a suitable online broker.

We want to feel secure with the peace of mind that our funds are in safe hands. Top brokers will invest a lot of money in updated software to protect the funds and data of their clients. In a world where there are new, improved methods of hacking, these companies are constantly updating their security software to stay ahead of the hackers. You can check on the security updates of the brokers and check information about the breach of their security software.

The Reputation of the Broker

Brokers rely on their reputation to land clients, and more than half of their clients are based on the reputation of the broker. Top brokers are those that have been doing business online for a number of years with a good record, and their long-time customers can testify to their reliability.

In most cases, we encourage newbie to go with a broker that has years of experience offering services to customers. This is because you may not want to trust your funds with a company that has no history. In researching brokers for trading options online, check for feedback by customers who have used the brokers. Search for brokers with a high percentage of positive reviews over a long period of time.

The reviews should be authentic because there are brokers who will buy positive reviews to create a fake impression. But, one way of avoiding brokers who play those tricks is to check out the consistencies in their feedback. It will be difficult for traders with a long history base to fake years of reviews, especially when they have a huge customer base.

You may also contact some of the users of these brokers to get information about the brokers. You can get information from a social group made up of traders, or from your mentor or from reliable sources. One way of getting authentic feedback about brokers is to use an independent review website, where clients will explain their real experience with a broker. Such websites may act as an unbiased base of getting feedback from real people.

During the course of this book, we are going to provide you with a list of some reputable brokers that you can feel safe trading with.

Regulated by Proper Authority

By law, financial institutions are regulated by a suitable financial body of the country they are registered to do business in. This is one way to ensure that the brokers you find are safe and that the broker is operating with the appropriate licenses.

Check that they have the proper regulatory permit, and they operate under the guidelines of a suitable monitor agency. There are dubious brokers who are not regulated and run some sharp practices that are against the guidelines of trade and protecting clients. Trading with an unregulated broker puts you at risk as they will have no obligation if you hold them responsible for unruly practices. But with a regulated broker, you will be protected by the regulator since the activities of the brokers are monitored.

Fast and Responsive Customer Service

At some point in time, you may encounter some difficulties in using the services of a broker, or you may need assistance at some point from the broker. You will want any issue you have in using the platform quickly resolved so you can get back to making money. Time is of the essence in trading, and you will want to get responded to in a timely manner and get your complaints attended to as fast as possible.

Before you sign up with a broker, ensure that you test their response time with their customer service department. Check the means through which you can contact the customer services if you can access them by phone, email, Skype, or through their social media platform. Ensure that they make use of as many means of communication as possible. I prefer using a broker that I can connect with through channels like phones, social media platforms, and emails. This is because these are the main means I can access the company online.

Before you sign up with a broker, you can place a call through to their customer services and check how long it takes to get a response. And you can then be sure of their ability to resolve problems fast, providing you with a knowledgeable solution.

Some brokers will take longer than usual in responding and resolving issues, or the customer representative does not have the knowledge to attend to the issues. Top brokers have experienced and knowledgeable people to respond to clients. They usually provide support in various languages to attend to customers all over the globe.

Well, you should understand that the issue of having access to responsive customer service is not the total deal. The customer services should be able to resolve your problem faster and be able to resolve the issue adequately. You can only determine the quality of the customer services from reviews by real customers or by asking technical questions and waiting to see how accurate their responses are.

In essence, when you are researching a company, you should check for the following based on customer services:

1. They have numerous means through which you can access them both online and offline. We should be able to access them through the phone, email, and social media.

2. They should be able to communicate with you in a language that you will understand. Ensure that the broker has several languages that they can communicate with their clients.

3. The customer services should be available 24/7 or during trading hours.

4. Check out the reviews related to their customer service online.

Availability of other financial instruments

You should understand that there are other financial instruments available that can make you money. To be honest, most traders diversify and trade other financial instruments such as shares or Forex, which also require brokers. It is best to go for a broker that offers other financial instruments on their platform. You can easily switch to trade other instruments that are available with the broker if you are into multiple trading.

Most brokers offer the option of trading these financial institutions, and it gives you the opportunity to have your funds secured with a broker you trust and save you the stress of having multiple trading accounts on your devices if you intend trading other financial instruments. Traders that use options as a hedge while trading other financial institutions will find such brokers useful with this trading style.

Ease of Deposit and Withdrawal

To trade options, you have to deposit funds into your account, and with a wide range of deposit methods available, make sure that the brokers have one you can easily use. Brokers use different methods for depositing funds, so ensure you check out the method available for you to deposit funds if they have the one you trust with your funds. We have so many transfer methods such as bank deposit, bank wire, PayPal, Skrill, credit cards, and so on, and check this out gives you a good idea of the best brokerage for your use.

You should note that some countries do not support some of these fund transfer systems, so make sure that your broker has the one that is convenient for you to transfer funds. The transfer agency should be fast enough to deposit your money, as most of them provide facilities for an instant deposit.

Now that we have deposited funds, the next consideration is how to withdraw your profit. This is the main reason we are trading; to make money, and we want to be sure that we can withdraw our money with ease. Before you register, check that the platform offers a suitable method for withdrawing your money. You should note that some of these methods of withdrawal are not accepted in some countries, so ensure that they use fund transfer methods that you can use to withdraw your money.

Check for Charges

Brokers have some hidden charges that you may not know about when registering to trade on their platform. You may find deposit or withdrawal charges when making transactions, including charges for other services. Some of these fees are normal with most brokers, but you should ensure that you are comfortable with these charges. Also, it is important to check these charges with other brokers to ensure that you are not being charged excessively.

Before signing up, research these charges and check with other brokers to compare. It is important that you minimize the charges on your account as much as possible. We are here to make money, and one way is to reduce the charges on these platforms.

Alternative Method of Making Trade

With the Internet, you can easily make a trade from your smartphone and have access to your brokers 24/7. However, there might be occasions when we have to place a trade based on the information we come across, and we may not have access to the Internet. On such occasions, you will be able to place a trade if you have alternative access to make a trade with your broker, such as the telephone.

Some brokers offer alternative methods such as phone calls to place a trade. You will put a call through to an account officer, provide your information to the account officer, and with your details, the officer can do the trade for you, making it easier. Such brokers usually provide alternative passwords or keys that you must provide to make a trade through the phone. The phone password is usually different from the password used in signing in to your trade platform, but this is for security reasons.

This may not be necessary, but it gives you an advantage to trade anywhere you are without an Internet connection. You will also be able to close a transaction, monitor transactions, and get help from your account officers.

Minimum Deposit Required

You might also want to consider the minimum deposit required for opening an account with a broker. As a beginner, you may want to consider starting with a small amount before investing big in the market. So you will go for a broker with the amount you have to deposit to test your trading skills.

The minimum amount required to deposit for some brokers is usually too high for some traders. In this situation, you will need to search for a broker that has a minimum deposit to accept the amount you have to invest in the beginning.

Incentives Offer by Brokers

There are so many brokers available on the market that the competition for clients has become a force. This is a huge advantage for traders as these brokers are now offering incentives to sign up and trade on their platform. The incentives may vary from cash bonuses on registration and deposit, to prizes that you can win when you participate in competitions.

Traders can take advantage of these incentives, especially cash bonuses, to increase their capital and make profits. A broker may give out 30% of each deposit that you can trade with, and this is a huge advantage for traders to increase their capital and in the same way, increase their leverage to make more money.

Before taking a big part with such brokerages, check the restrictions and other conditions attached to these incentives. It is important that you understand how they will affect your trading and profit before you enter the market.

I registered with a broker and was given free funds to trade with, and I was so happy. I spent some months trading on that account, increasing the fund to a substantial amount to the point I wanted to make a withdrawal. Now here comes the problem. I was told I could not make a withdrawal for that account until I made a deposit of some specific amount. I failed to read that point when it was stated that I should make a deposit of some specific threshold. In all, the time I invested in that account was a waste, and I could not get the money for the stipulated time to cash out on the bonus before it expired. So it is important to know the terms and conditions before agreeing to a bonus and trading on the account.

Trading Levels Available on the Platform

As we stated earlier, during the process of registration, you may be required to fill out some information that will determine your trading level on the platform. Being a speculative trader that wants to hedge your fund, you will be placed on a different level from one who wants to trade for profit.

It is then important to check for the level of traders available on the platform. Go for a broker that has the necessary trading levels so you can switch if the need arises.

In this chapter, we have shown you all you will need to consider when choosing a broker. It is important that you get it right with the broker you choose. The broker you use is essential for you to learn and make a profit, their services, and the assistance they provide to make it easier for you.

If you have a problem selecting a broker, go through the factors we have asked you to consider. However, we will be providing you with reviews of some of the brokers to trade with from our research. Make a note of them so you can tick the boxes as you check.

Chapter 3

Recommended Brokers for Option Trading

We have discussed how to select the right broker in the previous chapter, and we believe that will have been of help to our readers. To make things easier for you, which is the basis of this book, we are going to provide you with some recommended brokers.

Options trading is a kind of big risk investment, and we need a suitable broker to ease things for us as a trader. Our team has selected these brokers after thorough research based on what they have to offer and on reviews from customers. We will discuss the pros and cons of using these brokers so you can make a decision on the one that suits you.

You should bear in mind that we do not recommend any particular broker, but this is just a guide to direct you to some of the brokers you might want to try. On the other hand, based on the description on the platform, you may find useful ways of selecting a suitable broker as well.

Ameritrades

This is one of the top brokers for option trades, and they have everything for all kinds of traders. We would recommend these brokers for beginners as well as experts, no matter your level of trading. They do not have a minimum amount for opening an account, and a trade cost $6.95 with a commission of 0.75cents for each contract.

The advantage for beginners includes available resources to help beginners learn more about options trading. The broker is available to help you succeed and make a profit, providing clients with the needed resources at any level of trading. It is suitable for traders who do not have much to invest in their accounts. However, there are huge benefits and incentives for depositing a large amount of capital.

Presently, you can get a 60-day free commission on trading when you deposit $3000 or above as well as additional bonuses you can trade with on depositing huge amounts. Professional traders get information from Wall Street and other top news agencies to help them analyze the market.

Being a broker, they have a reliable customer service that you can call on at any time. The customer representative is knowledgeable about the market and can provide you with the needed help. The broker is recommended for beginners as well as professionals, and that is why it is our number one pick.

Robinhood

As a beginner with fewer funds to invest in the market, Robinhood is the best broker for you. They are designed for beginners with easy to use on the platform and no trade fee. The no-trade fee is one of the main catches with Robinhood, and that why it is highly recommended for beginners and those willing to try their knowledge of option trading after learning about it.

It offers low-risk trading to beginners and has a mobile and web platform for easy access to accounts and information by brokers.

However, they lack the resources that would be useful to experienced traders, but you can get those resources from somewhere else and use this platform to make your trade. They do not offer more services for experienced traders, and, from the reviews, most experienced traders are not happy about their methods of processing trades on the platform.

RobinHood also offers other financial instruments for trade, including cryptocurrencies, shares, and ETF on a no commission fee trade.

Highly recommend for beginners but does not offer more for experienced traders. With a high priority on its mobile platform, you can access your account on the go. Trade anywhere with this platform which is one of the major pros of using the platform.

Tradestation

For experts and those that trade high volume, Tradestation will offer you the best options and resources you can get from any other broker. This broker is not suitable for beginners, but for high volume accounts and for expert traders.

It asks for a $95 annual fee, which you can avoid by depositing at least $2000 and by opening more than five trades a year. Tradesations provide unlimited resources for traders, which will be useful for traders in making financial decisions in the market. With this broker, you get more incentives when you deposit more money and make more trades.

While I would advise those big-time traders to use this platform, it would not be suitable for a newbie, especially those who have limited funds to invest in the market. Besides, you will need experience in the market to be able to use the information and resources available on this platform. And in addition, most beginners would not have the kind of money to spend on certain fees on this platform.

Tradestation used to be a software company before they invested in the brokerage business. And they have one of the best software packages for trading while also offering their services to other companies.

Charles Schwab

As a beginner, Charles Schwab offers you the best educational resources to help you become a great trader. They have the resources to help both inexperienced and experienced traders, and the brokerage offers a wide range of platforms for trading, including web, desktop, and mobile. Trade on the go with their user-friendly platforms, which contain all you will need to trade successfully.

One downside for beginners is that it requires you to deposit a minimum of $1000, which is very high. The brokerage has a trade cost of $0.95, and the commission is $0.65, but you can get 50 commission-free commission trades for three years when you deposit $100,000 and above.

Charles Schwab also provides you with the options to trade and manage other financial instruments on the platform. You have the option to trade other instruments and manage several investments with this broker.

It is a nice broker for beginners with cheap transaction and commission fees but only for traders with substantial funds to invest. Being one of the platforms with vast educational resources in their library, you can educate yourself, acquire more knowledge, and enter the market like a pro. The broker will make you a better trader than you were when you joined if you make use of their resources.

Ally Invest

Looking for a broker with a low cost for transactions and the lowest minimum deposit, then Ally Invest is the best for you. Alley Invest, which is known as a top bank, opened a brokerage where you can trade options and enjoy some incredible incentives.

Being easy to use the platform, you can trade with a cost of $4.95 and $0.65 for commission. Although the price of the contract may be a little higher than those of other brokers, this will not be an issue as you can invest any amount you want since there is no minimum deposit.

You can enjoy great incentives and bonuses from this platform with up to $3000 available for grabs as a bonus with a solid platform, easy to understand charts, resources, data, and analysis to help you pick the best platform to trade.

I would recommend this broker for all traders for it has a lot to offer, and you can improve your trading using their platform. Although the charges for the transaction may be higher than some other brokers, it offers more, so don't be too bothered about the difference.

Interactive Broker

The interactive broker is only suitable for people who have a substantial amount to invest to enjoy its incentives. It is best for those that high trade volume and not just a few trades a year, for there is no transaction fee and commission as low as $0.70. However, the downside, especially for beginners, is that you will be required to make a deposit of $100,000 or to pay $10 amount as an activity fee.

Now there is a $20 charge on your account if you do not have a minimum of $20000 on your account. The charges seem to be very high, but for a trader that trades high volume, you can enjoy a commission for your trade as low as $0.15.

The cons of this broker include the excessive charges and the required minimum deposit, which is pegged at $100,000 to enjoy certain incentives. I would not recommend this broker for beginners or those who trade sparingly in options. Only high volume traders will enjoy the incentives offered on this platform, so anyone who has up to $100,000 to deposit can make use of the platform and enjoy great incentives

Lightspeed

The Lightspeed broker is suitable for experimental traders, and we would not recommend it for beginners. With expert tools available for traders, you can get the necessary support to make a huge volume of trade at a very low price. You can make transactions at a fee of $0.60 dollars. The platform is suitable for high trading volumes, and you can trade through the web, desktop, or mobile.

ETrade

ETrade is one of the oldest and trusted platforms for options trading for both beginners and experts. The cost of the trade is higher than you will get on other platforms at \$6.95 per trade at a commission of \$0.75. With their own trade platform known as the OptionHouse platform, this provides you access to charts and other analytical tools, which will provide support for your trades.

They will provide helpful tools and resources that will ensure your success in trading options. However, to enjoy huge incentives with this broker, you will have to deposit a huge amount of funds. With \$10,000, you will enjoy \$600 bonuses and 60 free trades that you can use to reduce the cost of trading options.

We have mentioned eight brokers with whom you can trade options with huge benefits, as discussed on each broker. Selecting a broker will be determined by the kind of trader you are and how much you will be trading. Now take a look at the advantages these brokers' offers and find the one that will offer you incentives that help you reduce the cost of trading.

Factors to Consider in Choosing a Broker

Capital

Capital is an essential part of investing in options, and your funds will determine the broker you will select. The amount you have to invest will determine the type of broker you will choose, while a trader with low funds will go for a broker with low deposit requirements. The trader may also want a broker that will have a low fee for trading to reduce the amount spent on the platform.

A trader with huge funds or capital can enjoy the benefits of using top brokers with massive benefits. Brokers that require a large deposit to open an account usually offer incentives such as a free commission for trading and cash bonuses that you can trade with on the platform. These bonuses can be used to increase the leverage for your trade, and you can trade more and increase your profit with these bonuses.

Well, if you are investing a considerable amount of money as the required deposit, you should also expect more from the broker. And that is why these brokers have expert analytical tools that will improve your trading skills.

Brokers that require no minimum deposits or very low deposits to operate their accounts do not have such incentives. They mostly don't offer premium services where traders can enjoy such benefits as expert advice and other tools required on the platform.

However, you must understand that all these resources may not be necessary to be a successful trader. Although they might be helpful, you can be successful with a basic knowledge of trading. A piece of advice to newbies would be to trade with brokers that offer no minimum or low deposit, and from there on, you can learn. With such brokers, you will be risking less and, as a beginner, it would be unwise to take on too much risk when you invest too much at the start.

As you gain experience and with profits made from using these low deposit brokers, you switch to one of the top brokers that require high capital for a minimum deposit. You will then enjoy such benefits as expert analytical tools and huge bonuses.

Your Experience in trading options

Brokers are keen to know your experience with online trading, and this will be used in classifying you on the platform. In choosing a broker, you have to consider your experience to be with a broker that will offer you the required help and assistance for your level of trading.

An experienced trader can understand and use expert analysis properly, so it will be convenient for the trader to use a platform that offers expert analysis. On the other hand, these analyses are not needed by someone who is just learning the scope of the market, as this will likely complicate trading for the trader. At this early stage, the trader will need more elementary support, which will be found in platforms that are beginner-friendly.

Check the resources available on a trading platform and check if they can be useful for a beginner. Are these resources elementary, and would you be able to understand the information and all that is required on this platform? As the trader begins to attain more experience and knowledge in trading, you may move to other brokers that offer more complex analyses to trade the market.

My advice to traders is to be patient in the process of learning how to trade as you begin with the elementary. This involves starting with a broker that has the resources to attend to a newbie. You can find an example of some brokers that suit this description in the list provided above.

Price of contract and commission fee

It is important to get the price of the contract and the commission fees all sorted out as you trade options. We are trying to reduce the amount we spend on trading, which can be regarded as money management, so we don't spend more than expected.

As a trader, we would like you to be conscious of the amount of risk on your capital as you get involved in a trade. This is why the price of the contract charged by each broker and the commission is an important aspect of our trading.

As a beginner, you will definitely go for ways to reduce costs regardless of the other benefits you may get from the broker. If you are a high volume trader, you will be looking for a broker that offers low prices to buy a contract as well as huge discounts offered on large-volume sales while choosing a broker with a lower price of contract and commission fees will be suitable especially for a beginner, brokers with a high price of trade and commission fees have their own benefits.

User-friendly trade platform

You have to understand that there are different trading platforms available for different brokers, and some have designed a unique trading platform. Now you do not want to get confused when trading options based on the reason that you cannot operate the platform. It may be difficult to find the buy or sell buttons on some platforms.

Either you are using a common platform, or you get used to the trading platform. A user-friendly platform will determine the speed and ease of executing contracts. While a trader may experience difficulty using an unfamiliar platform, some other platforms are just too difficult to trade on. They have features arranged in a way that will make it difficult for you to find what you want.

In another case, some brokers have developed their platforms, and this can be user-friendly, which is the basis of developing that platform in the first place. It is best that you get familiar with the platform as soon as you open the account. If possible, go through a tutorial class on how to use these platforms, so you do not risk your capital learning on the live market.

Mobile and web trading platform.

It is impossible to be on your computer all day, and when we are away from our computers, we may be interested in checking the markets. The application of a web platform and mobile platform will be of use in this market as you can move around with the market in your hands. These are one of the features that will suit the modern-day traders who move around a lot.

The web platform is suitable for checking your information and monitoring trades without having to download the platform on the system. You can access your platform from any computer with Internet access using the web application.

With mobile software, you have access to trade and information on the go. With the mobile application, you will never miss any opportunity to enter a trade and easily make trade decisions on your phone.

We have discussed brokers and their features, including the factors we considered when choosing the type of broker we should use. We are going to summarize all these points to consider for both inexperienced and experienced brokers for easy analysis.

For the inexperienced broker, you should consider the following factors in choosing a broker.

   i.   Low or no minimum deposit requirement so as to start with small capital.

  ii.   Access to resources that will help in locating basic knowledge of trading.

 iii.   User-friendly platform

 iv.   Low cost of trades and commission.

  v.   Good customer support.

 vi.   Flexible deposit and withdraw method.

 vii. Interactive platform

While for the experienced traders who may need more complex services than the inexperience traders would consider a broker with the following:

1. Support for expert analyses

2. Have incentives for high volume traders

3. Offer commission and bonuses for a huge deposit of funds.

4. They may have a dedicated trade platform.

5. Fast and responsive platform.

6. Options to trade other financial instruments.

Chapter 4

The Terminology of Option Trading

In options trading, there are some specific terminologies that a trader must know to be able to understand what is going on in the market. These terminologies are used by traders to discuss their experience in analyzing the market with other traders.

You will also find these terms used in market analysis, and being unfamiliar with them will leave you confused and cut out of the conversation. We are going to list out the common terminology used in option trading

Option: the options are contracts that are set to buy or sell a designated amount of stock at a certain price with an expiration date.

Strike Price: this is the set price at which we are going to sell or buy the contract. You are to set the trade to trigger at the strike price, and we wait until the expiration date to see if we make a profit or loss with the trade. The strike price is the price per share, and this will be multiplied by the total amount of shares you buy when the market hits the set price. In some cases, strike prices are regarded as exercise prices, and it is important to analyze this price to make a profit with your trade

Call Option: with a call option, a buyer will buy 100 shares of the stock when it meets the requirement of the strike price. With the call option, you are buying a contract with the hope that the contract will rise in the market.

Put Option: this is the opposite of a call option, and it involves the sale of a specified amount of the stocks when it hits the strike price during the expiration period. Simply put, we can say that we are selling, while with the call we are buying.

The Writer: The writer is the seller that will sell the required amount of stock to the buyer when the strike price is activated on the platform.

Exercise: this is the process in which the contract is now in play, and the strike price has been triggered. Any contract that is in the money will be triggered; that is, any contract with at least a cent on it will get into play and be exercised at this point.

The Expiration Date: this is the last day in which the contract can be triggered, and once it is not triggered within the last day, then the contract will no longer be in play.

Hedging: This is a common term in the market that is used to minimize risk as you take a trade in the opposite direction of an existing share or stock. This is a strategy used by huge investment companies to reduce the risk of an already losing position.

Covered Call: this is a call position that has been sold or in more technical terms that have been written. This transaction will be triggered when a call option that is in play.

Intrinsic Value: the intrinsic value is the profit that is expected from a contract, which is either a put or a call. A contact that is in profit is regarded as In the Money ITM, and when in loss, it is referred to as Out Of The Money OTM. An example will be that the intrinsic value of 100 shares of a stock is $2, and it is currently trading at 34.56 dollars; the intrinsic value will be the profit displayed by how much the price has moved over $34.56 from the entry.

Time Value: the time value, on the other hand, is the added amount to the intrinsic value. As in the example above, if the value of the trade with a call price of $4 at $34.56, then the time value is $2. While if the call option is out of money, then the time value will be considered as the market value of the trade.

Premium: the premium is the total cash value of the asset, and this can be calculated by the multiplication of the price per share by 100 shares.

Premium= price per share x 100 shares

Time Decay: options are traded with an expiration date, and as the date gets closer, the time of that contract decays. So as we draw closer to the date of expiration of the contract, the options time decay increases.

Long: we go long when we buy an option in an open transaction and hold a position for the option.

Short: we go short when we sell an option in an opening transaction.

Long Term Equity Anticipation Securities LEAPS: these are securities that are bought on a long-term deal that can last up to three years.

The above are the most common terms you will find in trading options and come across in discussion groups. They are simple to understand, and as you trade regularly, you will understand the meaning and begin to use them freely.

You will also come across more technologies as you get trading, but with the above terms, you are good to start your trade.

Types of Traders and Their Trading Style

In a broad sense, we can classify traders into inexperienced and experienced traders, which is put into simple terms. But when it comes to styles and patterns of trading, we can also classify traders into four groups. As you get to understand more about options trading, you will notice that, just like other financial instruments, they require some similar trade skills and patterns.

We are going to classify option traders into four based on the length of time that the traders hold their trades and their style of trading.

The Day Traders

The day traders are active on the market, watching how the market moves all day and waiting for opportunities to enter the market and make a profit. With day traders, they open positions and closed positions on the same day.

It is a time-consuming style and usually practiced by professionals, although used by private individuals who have all day to study how the market moves. The day traders trade at least once a day, and they can have more than two positions per day depending on their trading style and how long they have to study reading the market.

Swing Traders

Those that do not have the time to stay and study the market all day but want to catch in on some fast moves in the market. Swing traders open a position and may leave it for a longer time than the day trader, and they do not have to spend all day watching the market.

Swing traders trade much larger moves than day traders, and they capture a large volume of moves in the market. They are another class of a set of traders who will find trading financial instruments in a longer time frame and with less stress.

Swing trading is suitable for beginners for the following reasons:

i. With swing trading, the trader has enough time to analyze the market and plan their trade. Unlike day trading, which is quite intense, spending all day reading charts and other analyze.

ii. You have more opportunities than being a long-term trader and can trade all day or week.

iii. The potential for making more trade increases the chances of making money.

Position Traders

Position traders are those big investors who are working in top financial institutions that are not ready to be on the market all day. They make trades that last for more than a day, and that can even run for weeks. This style of trading is for experienced traders, and those who have considerable capital can make profits over one or two days.

This style of trading can be frustrating for beginners who will have fewer opportunities to trade. In comparison to other financial instruments, this kind of trading is common with traders trading options, but with experienced options traders.

Market Makers

The fourth category of options traders is the market makers who are top financial traders or investors with a very considerable sum of capital. These market makers can move liquidity in the market as they usually trade in high volume.

These are employees of top financial institutions, and with the high volume of trade in the market, they determine how the market moves. These market makers are available to buy and sell options, even when the volatility of the market is low.

Chapter 5

The Techniques of Trading Options with Fundamental Analyses

O ptions trading involves analyzing the movement of the market, the direction or no direction of the market. Options involve predicting where the market will move, easy as it may sound; this will involve analyzing the market with the right parameters.

This begs the question, what moves the market, and how can we follow these parameters to predict the next move of the market?

You must have watched CNN, BBC, CNBC, or other top world news channels during breaking news that affects the markets. At times you may wonder about some unrelated business news driving markets as the new analyst begins discussing how some political or natural disasters have driven the market up or down.

Yes! Natural disasters such as earthquakes, wildfires, floods, and hurricanes usually affect the market and may drive stock prices high or low in huge volumes. This news affecting the market is known as the fundamentals of trading the market. However, no one can predict such disasters to take a position before they happen and make huge profits.

War and famine are other factors that will affect the stock market adversely or the death of top political leaders. In the United Kingdom, the birth of a royal or the Queen celebrating a milestone can favor the British economy. So good or bad news also affects the market in unpredictable ways and manners, as investors rush to take positions in the market.

Also, business deals between big companies or the acquiring of one company by another also have an effect on stock prices, and investors can take advantage of these volatile moves in stock prices. All these news events are regarded as fundamentals that drive the market, and they usually occur in high volume, especially those high impact news.

Options traders can find opportunities to enter the market and make some money with this breaking news. That is why you find most traders always check on what is happening globally, especially when it affects countries like the United States, China, Japan, Germany, and countries that have a major role to play in the world economy.

In 2004, one of the biggest earthquakes recorded hit Japan and affected the global stock market, moving irrationally. Stock prices across America and Asia fell sharply, and there was an adverse effect on the price of oil following the disaster. The disaster also affected stock prices in India and Sri Lanka even though the prices later normalized after a day or two.

Another major disaster that caused huge economic impact, especially in the United States, was Hurricane Katrina that affected New Orleans in 2005. This affected the United States economy with the loss of over 400 000 jobs and the cuts in oil production, which resulted in a fall in the dollar and stock prices.

From these two disasters mentioned, there were adverse effects on the market with high volatility with the impact the news had on the market. Options traders can take advantage of these sharp moves in the market to predict the movement of the prices of shares. These are high impact news situations that drive the market, and options traders can make money either way as long as the volatility is high.

The situations discussed above are unexpected news, and their moves in the market are fast. In the financial market, there are some fundamental parameters that can be used to trade options and other financial instruments. These are fundamental news that can be released at a certain period, and they have a huge impact on the market. Traders look forward to the time this news will be delivered so they can take advantage of the impact on the market to make huge moves.

Options traders can trade on this fundamental news, and the process is known as a fundamental method of trading options. When this high impact news is released, traders will be on standby from the time the news is released and use the data or information of the news to predict the direction of the market.

There are several financial news programs aligned to be released every week, and you can find this information online. Check on financial platforms like the Forex factory to know when this news will be released. One reason I like using the Forex factory is that they indicate which news is important and which has low impact. High impact news is indicated with red, and when this news is being released, you will expect high volatility in the market. On this platform, you get an analysis of what the market might do and the expected data that will be added to the market. With this analysis, you can predict where the market will likely be heading when the high impact news hits the market.

I like using this high impact news to predict how stocks will move and how the market will react. With proper analysis and based on where you think the market will be heading in the near future, you can catch a good ride on prices in the market. It is easy to trade the news with options, for you only need to predict the direction the market is going in without waiting for the price to reach its target.

It is usual for the United States economy to improve when there is an announcement that there is an increase in the number of people employed that month. Of course, there is a high probability that stock prices will go higher with this favorable data, and, in most cases, buying an option will yield profit in such a situation.

News that you can use for Proper Fundamental Analysis

We have some important news coming up that will have a high impact on the market. It will cause high volatility in the market during that period. What we do when trading using fundamentals is to search for high or medium impact news. There is no point in trading low impact news, for when this is released, it rarely causes high volatility movements in the market.

So we are going to look out some of the high impact news that you should read and show you how you can trade using the news. Take note that not all news is important or drives the market as you would want them to drive the market. There are some news releases that are expected to cause huge volatility in the market that will come up regularly on the market calendar.

Trading of news is known as fundamental analysis, and, as a trader, I set my alarm to be aware of these important news items coming up. Most of them are financial reports of some of the top companies in the world. Like you would expect, there could be a big move in the market when the United States financial institutions are set to make an announcement about the economy. Investors will be waiting by the sideline to get the information and input that information into the market while small-time traders will be waiting to see how the big investors and the market react to the news and take advantage of the trend in the market.

There are some investors and institutions that can direct the flow of the market, while traders like us use the historical reaction of this news to predict the market. If you are new to fundamental analysis, I would like you to do some back-testing on when important news was released on the market and the huge impact it had on volatility. The good thing about trading financial instruments is that we have a backlog of information that you can study from using your charts.

Just go to the chart on any broker's website and move back to check on the dates of high impact news, and you will realize the huge force it had on the market. I know traders that are only available on their platform to trade news releases.

Now I am going to list out some of the important news that you can trade with successfully on options trading based on research.

The Non-Farm Payroll

The nonfarm payroll is one of the news releases fundamental traders lookup every month, and it is released on the first Friday of each month. The non-farm roll is the number of people that gained employment in the economy of the United States, and it is one of the highest impact news items on the market. This report can send the market in waves in any direction, depending on how favorable the news is to the economy.

Because of its high volatility, some traders who are core fundamental traders will trade only when this report is released. This is because they are sure that the market will be active, and they can predict the direction of the news. Traders are happy when the market is active, and this is one of the periods we have a huge amount of traders watching the news and ready to dive in to take advantage of the high impact news.

You may be asking yourself, why is the non-farm report so important?

Many traders will not be able to answer this question, mainly because they do not care and are just happy to see the market move so fast. But to help you understand how you can take advantage of this report, which will help you predict the right direction, we are going to shed light on the importance of this report.

The economy of the United States is the biggest in the world, and the global markets respond to whatever is happening in this economy. A rise or drop in the value of the dollar will affect other major currencies like Euro, Yen, Aussie, and the Pound. So this will affect shares, stock, and commodities in all the major economies in the world and determine the direction of stock and share prices. So those economists who understand the impact of such major moves in the market can quickly take a position in anticipation of the movement in the market based on the report that was just released.

With the nonfarm payroll report, we are getting the number of people who gained employment in the previous month. And this report will tell us how the economy of the United States fares in the previous month, which we can use to anticipate the health of the economy and predict the direction of the market.

So in anticipating the moves, we can predict a rise or fall in certain options based on this report. I can say with options trading; it can be easier as we predict a certain directional move in the market based on the state of the economy.

There are different ways that traders can use the Non-Farm Report to trade. We can predict the daily movements of the market, the monthly move, or move on a higher time frame based on this report. So, in essence, how you use the report will depend on the kind of trader you are: day trader, swing trader, position trader, or market maker.

When you do not have much impact on the market, you can take advantage of the daily move to predict the direction of the trade.

Before the release of such impact news, there are speculations by top financial advisers on what the actual result will be and how it can impact the market. Before the release of the result, some traders may have set their options based on the expected outcome and the anticipated movement of the market.

These speculators make use of information available to them and historical data to predict the movement of the market. Based on activities during the month, they are able to analyze the market and expect that the report may fall as anticipated and analyze the direction of the market. Traders who follow some of these top analysts will set trades based on the anticipated moves and hope that it triggers in their direction. And if it does, they will have made a huge profit with the moves, although they are not right all the time.

The report might also be very different from the anticipated moves and move against them in the market. And this is why most people wait for the news before entering the market or setting their trade as they anticipate the result. Speculators may be wrong, and placing a trade based on speculation is not an ideal move because the move is highly unpredictable.

However, we would encourage traders to understand how the release of this news will affect the global market and will impact your trading. As an options trader, looking forward to the actual release of the data will determine the direction you will take on the market. Although we are all speculating the move of the market, speculative trading is usually more far-fetched than basing your move on actual news and can be confusing.

Listening to the analysis on cable news such as CNN, CNBC, and so on trying to guess and tell us the next move in the market can be exhausting. Although I find these news releases informative, I would advise you to avoid making important trade decisions based on most of these speculators. Learn how to trade the market with the news that comes as a result of this report.

The United States Non-Farm Payroll report will tell us the health of the economy, which we can use to analyze shares, stock, and commodities. A good report indicates that the economy is improving and will have a positive impact on global shares and stocks, which will see investors being confident in the market and a corresponding rise in share prices. When the news comes out good, like there is an increase in employment, as an options trader, it will be a good time to predict the upward movement of some shares, and I can buy stocks anticipating their upward movement over a certain period of time.

With the health of the economy in good shape, investors are happy and will invest more, so we expect stocks and share prices to rise, which is a good indicator to take a position in some stocks and share options.

While, on the other hand, a drop in the employment rate or a negative Non-Farm Payroll report will have a negative impact on the global economy. Investors become wary and try to secure their investments in safe havens like gold and other commodities. We experience a drop in the prices of shares and stock as the market reacts to the negative Non-Farm Payroll report. During this period, we may witness high volatility in commodities like gold, so when such reports come out, we can anticipate the move based on historical events.

With a negative result, we can move away from stock or predict that they will fall over a certain time with our options. In such cases as an investor in an options trade, you can layout plans to invest in gold, which will be rising with high volatility and take advantage of this period.

The result of the Nonfarm Payroll can have a huge effect through the months as investors react to the news. So this is where long-term traders can use the report to anticipate huge movement and take advantage of the report.

For your options trading, you should check how the market had behaved in previous days when the Nonfarm results were released. The Internet has made it possible for us to access such information and check history. Some traders place the trade once a month on this nonfarm report and take their profit while they wait for the next report. It suits the method of some traders, especially when your method requires the market to move, and you take a position - either up or down. With Non-Farm report out, we do not expect a ranging market, so it is not suitable for those who trade on range strategy.

You can find your own strategy to trade the Nonfarm Payroll report, and as you are learning this method, watch out for the news and how it affects the global market. Now before you start trading this market, you will need some time to study the market reaction to the news. If you can get your hands on old clips on YouTube on the daily analysis of markets during the release of the report, that will be good.

Just watch how the market figures move sharply as the result filters out; the figures on the board will keep moving sharply. This is due to traders making frantic efforts to buy or sell shares and stocks based on the data from the release. Learn how to read and anticipate these moves and take advantage of this news.

You should note that certain factors happening during the release of this report might also have an effect on the market. Some of these factors include:

- Global disasters happening during the time of the release may affect the way the market might react to the news.

- Celebration of top events such as ceremonies involving royalty like the Queen of England.

- High impact political news like elections, a proclamation of war, or other political events in the world.

- Business news like mergers, fraud, the breakup of companies, bailouts involving top economies and business.

- Social events such as the Olympics, World Cup, and other events.

All these happenings may have an effect on how the report affects the market, especially when they are happening at the same time. So it is not that easy to analyze the market based on just the Nonfarm Payroll report. You have to be able to make other considerations for other financial factors that will affect the economy at that particular time of the release.

I have noticed at some times when the report has been positive to the economy, but the market reacts in a different way. This may be due to other economic factors like political happenings, social events, and other disasters happening in the country like the Tsunami that happened in Japan in the year 2004. That month was a very difficult month for the global economy. The positives news result may not really provide any substantial improvement in the economy as investors may still be avoiding putting money into the economy. So a positive report will likely drive down the currency deeper than you would have expected.

Hurricane Katrina was another example of how positive news on the economy fails to react as would have been expected. Investors were on the sideline and seeking a safe haven with gold as there was a major dent in the economy of the country. With the supply of oil down and many people out of a job, any kind of positive result from other areas or sectors of the economy failed to make a positive impact on the economy.

So you should be able to analyze what is generally happening and how they will be affected in the news to take advantage and use it to benefit in your market dealings.

The Interest Rate by the Central Bank

Another important item of news I love to follow for my fundamental analysis of the market is the interest rate. The interest rate is the rate at which borrowers will pay to the bank for funds, and it is closely watched by investors to determine the health of the economy.

The Central Bank of a country usually meets at a certain time to determine the interest rate, reviews it, and determines what it should stand at, during a particular time. One of the reasons the interest rate is very important is that it will have an effect on the economy for a long time. The Central Bank has the capacity to increase the interest rate, decrease it, or keep it at the same rate depending on the economic situation at the time. Certain factors must be considered in determining the interest rates, and this is what they will do to improve the economy.

As we have said, the interest rate can have a huge impact on the economy of a country, and important interest rates to follow are those of the United States, the European Union, Japan, and the United Kingdom. The interest rates are closely watched by investors, as this will determine interest to investors to invest in a company. It will determine the growth of the economy as people will be willing to borrow money from the bank and invest in the economy.

What I look for when using interest rates as the fundamental analysis is how changes will impact the economy and the market. At times, the economy may need to have the interest rate increased or decreased, but the Central Bank might decide to keep the interest rate the way it is, and this may not favor the economy and may drive investors' sentiment down. In this case, the likely analysis is that the stocks will go down, and you can place your options to sell the stocks.

In most economical calendars, the interest rate is a high impact news item and marked red on the calendar. Traders and investors pay keen interest in the release of this information, and this will influence foreign investors and encourage people to invest in the economy. And you know what happens when more investors are tripping into the economy or a company. There will be expansion, and the likely growth of the share or stock prices will go up as investors become interested in that particular stock because of the favorable economy. And with the anticipated profit to be made based on expansion, people will become more willing to take a loan to raise capital and invest in the economy.

With a positive view of the economy, when the interest rate is released, and it favors the investors, you will want to buy options that the stock or shares that relate to that economy will rise. Going through speculation by expert professionals will guide you into choosing the right place to be on the market when the news is released.

Naturally, high-interest rates are favorable to investors, and this will drive the economy of the country high, especially the currency of that country. While the reverse is the case of the low-interest rate of the country and it will reduce the value of the currency and drive share prices lower

But, there are some scenarios where the interest rates are left unchanged when expected to be changed, and this may drive the market in another direction. That is why you have to pay attention to the present state of the economy and how the interest rate will affect the market at that instant.

Now we are going to discuss how to make money on **interest rate options**, which is investing in the rise and fall of the interest rate with the options broker. The interest rate option is a financial derivative offered by options brokers that will allow traders to invest their money on the changes in the interest rate. Some traders only trade the interest rate as they speculate based on economic analysis the direction of the interest, which makes a huge move based on the information of the market. With option trade, you can either put or call on the interest rate at the strike price towards an expiration date.

When investors believe that the interest rate will be increased, the buyer can set a buy option that the interest rate will increase at the expiration date. At the end of the expiration date, the buyer will have gained if the interest rate was higher at a price enough to pay the premium. This is one way of trading the interest rate option in the online market.

On the other hand, if the investors believe that the interest rate will fall, they will place a put option on the interest rate option on the platform at the expiration date. At the expiration date, the price of the premium is above that of the strike price, and then the seller would have gained in the market.

However, if at the end of the expiration date, the option fails to attain its predicted price, that is, it is below the price for a call option or above the strike price for put options, then you would have lost your investment. With this in mind, one has to follow the right strategy to ensure that you get it right and make a profit in the trade.

At some point, the investor might decide to execute the trade at the value at that price and settle with cash, and this is known as the spot yield.

Now we are going to show you an example of an interest rate option by buying the option in participation that the interest rate will increase. So let's assume that we are buying a contract at $50, which is the strike price. Let's assume that the call option was sold at $1, and we are going to buy 100 shares, which will now amount to $200.

Now at the expiration of the contract, the price of the interest rate option has risen to $60, which is $10 difference from the original price. We have paid $100 as the premium price for the call option, and to make a profit, the price at the end of the contract must be above this premium price. But at the end of the contract, there was a $10 difference from the original price, and we are now at $1000 in profit. But in the end, we will pay out the $100 we paid for the premium, and our profit now stands at $900.

You can see how profitable this trade can be, for we have invested $100 in the trade. And since it moved in our favor, we have made $900, risking just $100.

However, when the contract expires, and it did not move in your favor, then you would have lost out on $100. At this stage, the contract is termed Out of the Money, which is a terminology we discussed earlier in the past chapters.

This is not as easy as we discussed above, and you will need to be able to calculate the expected move in the market.

Commodity Investors Using Fundamental Analysis

Trading commodities can be easy with fundamental analysis and will be profitable with options trading using fundamentals in the market. Gold, silver, copper, and other major commodities move in the market based on news and other happenings in the world.

The prices of gold usually surge after there is a great demand for the commodity, especially when investors are nervous. Gold is regarded as a safe haven in the financial market when there are uncertainties in the market, and we can trade gold using options.

There are instances when it is better to trade gold as you can detect that the commodity will rise and go higher in the near future. Commodities can also be traded when there is high impact news as you can easily detect that the prices will either fall or rise based on the economic situation.

We have discussed some disasters that happen in the world, such as the Tsunami that happened in Japan and Hurricane Katrina. These disasters set uncertainty in the market as traders could not predict the direction of the market, and they were nervous about investing. In such cases, the market lacks direction as traders could not fathom the direction of the market or the future of the market.

Also, during elections or changes in government, there may be uncertainty as to where the direction of the economy might go, and investors will turn to gold as a safe haven. As you can see, there are certain situations and circumstances in the market that will need you to take gold as an option to trade.

You can call an option for gold when you realize that there will be huge volatility in the market due to uncertainties created by the news. Another case I would prefer to call an option on gold is when the Non-Farm Payroll result does not come out as expected and when traders do not know how the news will affect the market, expect commodities like gold to rise. On such a day that the news did not come out as expected, you can take a call option on gold to expire at the end of the day, as you take out some profit for the day.

Trading Oil with Fundamentals

Oil is another commodity that drives the economy, and the fall and rise of the prices of oil can be determined by the market. Oil is in high demand, and big economies like the United States, China, and other industrialized nations have a high demand for oil. The prices of oil are connected with supply and demand, which is driven by the economies and in some cases, by politics. The price of oil can go up when there is a reduction in the supply of the commodity which can arise due to war, politics, damage to oil facilities in oil-producing countries, or when OPEC decided to cut supplies.

In the case of politics, oil prices fell sharply after they lifted sanctions on Iran, which was one of the top oil-producing countries. With the lifting of the sanctions, there will be an expected surplus of oil in the market, and thus smart traders would have cut options on oil for a period of time. We saw the price of oil fall down way below $30 per barrel after the Iranian oil hit the world market. This is an example of how politics drives the oil market on a global scale and how options traders can take advantage of news releases to make money oil option derivatives.

In another case, an industrialized nation that demands oil on a large scale may decide that they want to switch to other energy sources like renewable energy. This news release will drive oil prices down as there will be fewer buyers for the product, and investors would choose to put their money elsewhere. In this case, taking a put option on oil in the near future would be a wise move to make some profit in the long run.

OPEC, which is a body that is made up of oil-producing countries, might decide to cut down oil production across the country, and this may affect the oil market. At the break of such news, we will be expecting oil prices to spike up in the near future as this will create some kind of scarcity in the market. Taking a put option will be wise at this point to make a profit on the market in the future.

Oil prices also fluctuate when there is political tension in some of the top oil-producing countries, like what happened in Saudi Arabia in 2019. Due to the tension in the Middle East and the war in Yemen, rebels attacked oil facilities in Saudi Arabia, bombing some huge oil storage tanks. The attack caused a sharp rise in the price of the commodities as people anticipated a reduction in the supply of oil in the market. Taking advantage of such a move will earn you some gain as you make a call option on oil to last for a short period of time.

Oil is very important for energy consumption, and any news that will affect the price of oil will affect a sharp move in either direction. This is why fundamental analysis of oil is another way to make money on options trading, especially when the news affects some of the top producers and consumers of oil.

The United States is a top producer and exporter of oil, and news on oil affects the economy of the country. Also, the relationship of the United States with top oil-producing countries does influence oil prices, as can be seen with their relationship with Saudi Arabia and Iran.

Advantages of Trading with Fundamental Analyses

Fundamental analysis is one of the ways of trading financial instruments, although not many are conversant with this analysis. If you understand the process of trading with this type of analysis, you can reduce your chances of losses with fundamental releases.

At this point, we are going to list out some of the advantages of trading with fundamentals, and they include:

- You will not over trade with fundamental analysis as you will be online to make a trade when there is high impact news.

- With fundamental analysis, there is a reason for each trade, which puts you in a good position to make correct decisions.

- The news causes high volatility in the market, which gives you a high probability of getting the right direction of your trade at the time the contract expires.

- You get prepared to trade since you are aware of the time the market will make a move.

- With fundamentals, you can get an idea of where the market will be heading with expert analysis.

The disadvantages of using fundamental analyses include:

- You will need to have a deep understanding of how the market reacts to fundamental news to trade options and make a profit.

- The news may be highly unpredictable, and it may move in any direction with the slightest change in data.

- It is hard for a newbie to trade with fundamentals.

- You can go days without trading.

Chapter 6

Trading Options with Technical Analyses

Technical trading involves the use of technical tools to predict the movement of the market without regard to the news. With technical analysis, you will be reading the charts to find out when the market is about to make a huge move and in what direction.

There are so many technical tools, but not all of them can give you the direction and momentum of the market. With option trade, we are concerned about the market moving in three patterns, and they are:

- Upward movement.

- Downward movement

- And side movement which is a proper term is referred to as range

The aim of using the technical indicators is to point the direction of the market or the lack of direction of the market as the case may be when in a range.

The method of trading options derivatives with technical indicators is different when using these indicators because with Forex and other financial instruments; you can hold the position indefinitely. However, with options, you have a limited time, which is the time decay factor with options. Your trade will expire on the date you set it when placing the option, so you will need an indicator that will determine a huge move in the market.

Such an indicator that will determine the volume of trade and tell you when a trend is about to begin and when the trend ends. With options, it is better to trade a derivative when a trend is about to commence, and you can set your expiration date based on the time chart you are using to analyze the market.

To trade options, the best indicators are those that tell us the momentum of the market. With these indicators, you can determine when the market is overbought, and when it is oversold. When you determine this, you will wait for the right opportunity to enter the market through the call or pull options.

Unlike fundamental analysis, with technical analysis, you see the reason why you want to take that position. With so many technical indicators available on the trading platform, only a few of these can actually give us what we want to achieve with options trading.

We are going to discuss some of the technical indicators, and most of them are momentum indicators that will be helpful in trading options derivatives.

Relative Strength Index RSI

This is one of the best indicators used by technical indicators use in trading stock and checking if a trend has come to an end or a new trend is about to begin. When a newbie begins to learn about technical trading, this is one of the most popular indicators they get to use for learning about the market.

The relative strength index, which is known as RSI, has a value of 0-100 attached at the bottom of the chart. It is not a chart indicator, so it does not disrupt the chart, giving you a clear chance to analyze the chart with the indicator.

Now, this indicator can be used to read a chart, and for a newbie, it is not too difficult to understand. I use it to trade stock, for it is perfect, giving us a precise direction of the market. In trading stock using RSI, we want to determine the momentum of the market if it is overbought or oversold, and this will determine the direction we will take in the market.

Now, in using this indicator, once the range is above 70, that means that the market is overbought and any signal that the market will go up is false and, at this point, we are looking at where the trend of the market will change.

The other point we will be looking at is when the market is below the 30 marks, and at this point, the market is oversold, and we will avoid any opportunity to sell in the market.

Now I like using the Relative Strength Index to determine the trend direction of the market, and this will give you a clear view of when to enter the market. Trading against the trend can give you false signals in most cases, which will result in a high loss in the market.

Now, if we know the dominant trend of the market, we can use this to enter the market and make money. If we have the stock market in an upward trend, we will wait for the relative strength index to fall below the 30 mark line in the RSI and then take a position that the stock will close high at a particular timeframe, which will determine our expiration date. If we are reading a chart based on an intraday time frame such as 15 minutes to 1 hour, then our expiration date might be the end of the day as we take in a call option for the trend.

If you are using a higher timeframe such as a 4-hour time-frame and above, you may want to extend the expiration date to more than a day and up to a month as we use a higher timeframe. The time frame to be used will determine the kind of traders we are, such as the day trader, swing trader, or the long-term trader.

For taking put position, you should ensure that the trend is downward and that the Relative Strength Index is reading above 70 and that it is overbought, so there is no going higher for the stock. And when it hits the mark of 70, then we can take a put position for the contract to expire at a time based on the time frame we are using in analyzing the market.

As you can see, this indicator gives direction to the market, and with this, you can easily plan your trade without any emotion. The relative strength index is suitable for trending positions and not for predicting range markets. With this indicator, you should be able to predict that a stock will go higher or lower than the strike price in the market.

In summary, we are to buy the security or call option when the market is oversold, and the RSI is below 30, while you should find an opportunity to short the market or put options when the market is above 70 on RSI. So take this into consideration when trading stock in the financial market with the timeframe in mind to consider your expiration date.

Using Bollinger Bands to Analyze Option

Another useful indicator for options trade that will determine volume in the market is the Bollinger band. This indicator is an envelope, and we are going to analyze the direction of the market on how the price reacts with the envelope or band. In this indicator, we have a higher boundary and lower boundary, and on most occasions, the price moves within this envelope or band.

To trade options using this indicator, we have to consider how the price reacts in the envelope and when it tries to move away from the envelope. Now, this indicator gives us the momentum of the market, and it can determine if the market is at a range, overbought, or oversold.

When the envelope is thin, that is, the upper boundary and lower boundary are close together, then the volatility of the market is low, with the market having no preferred direction, or we can say not trending and at a range.

Now, as the upper hand and the lower band begins to expand and move away from each other, we can agree that the volatility of the market is beginning to rise. And as it expands more, we can analyze where the chart or price is heading to in determining the trend. One simple trick you can use with this indicator is that the upper and lower band of the envelope act as resistance and support for the stick prove.

So when price engages the upper band, we can assume that the stock is approaching the resistance and will likely fall very soon. We can expect a deep in price when the candle or price begins to break above the upper band. At this instance, we will be taking the put option as we envision the price to drop within a day if you are trading the intraday time frame and take more than one day if you are trading using 4 hours' time frame and above. When the price moves below the lower band, then we will be expecting a reversal of the trend, and the momentum for downward movement is weak. At this stage, the stock price will not go down much as we are expecting a big move upward and a bullish trend to happen very soon.

You can begin to look for opportunities along with candle formation for an upward movement as the downtrend begins to weaken. The new trend may last for the whole day for intraday traders and may exceed a day when you are using the 4 hours and above timeframes.

The Bollinger band offers us a huge advantage to enter the market at a lower price so we can take full advantage of the move when it starts. The indicators will alert us at the time a new trend is about to form when the old trend is rounding up. With this indicator, you will enter the market at the right time when the price is very low or very high as the case may be, depending on the price of the market.

With option trade, we are not concerned about reaching a particular target, but that the price of the market is higher than the strike price and in profit to be able to cover our premium price. So with this in mind, we want to make a strike price to be at the beginning of the trend so that the market price would have risen way above the strike price, which puts you at a high advantage in the market.

So the Bollinger band allows you to enter the market at a good price and also determines that we are going to have enough volume to guarantee that our trade is safe and we enter at the lowest price possible.

Another way we can use Bollinger band to trade option derivatives is to trade a range market. We can predict that the market may not move past a certain price at the end of the day. We can achieve this when the Bollinger band begins to thin out after it has widened following a long trend. With this indicator, we can avoid buying the stock when the market is overbought, and buyers are getting out. Also, we will avoid predicting a fall when oversold, and buyers are about getting to the market.

You can see that this indicator is easy to understand; it will give you plenty of opportunities to enter the market and make money.

Intraday Momentum Index IMI

In a bid to make it easy for traders to interpret moves in the market using the charts and combinations of formulas to determine the trend in the market, the IMI was developed. The Intraday Momentum Index helps the intraday trader to predict the movement of the market. It works like the relative strength index with interpretation using the combination of chart movement.

The indicator is for intraday traders, and it will guide you on the trend to follow for the day. It is simple to read, and all the calculation has been made based on a number of days, the default being 14 days to analyze where the market will be heading to during the day.

IMI = the sum of up days is divided by the sum of up days plus the sum of down days x 100

The default number of days is 14 days, while a trader can edit the indicators to a number of days they are comfortable with to trade.

The intraday momentum index gives us a true picture of the intraday trends, and it will guide us when the bull or bear is coming to an end and when likely they will come to play at high volatility. Just like the RSI, this indicator tells us when the price of the market is at an overbought or oversold zone. With this guide, we can set to enter a downtrend move when the market has been saturated with buyers and is becoming fed up. At this stage, you will identify that the downtrend is about to begin, and we will look for the opportunity for the bear market and enter accordingly.

We look for this overbought region around the 70 marks of the IMI, just like the relative strength index. And just lie the RSI, the oversold zone is around 30, and at this stage, we are looking for a point to enter the market.

Also, it is important to get the predominating trend of the stock and trade according to that trend. You are placing yourself at a good stand to make a profitable trade when you trade along with the overbearing trend. As an intraday trader using this intraday method, you can check out the daily trend so that you will be on a safer side when you take a position.

If the daily trend is bullish, we will look to enter the market when it is oversold and be aligned to the major trend to make the right impact. When you are trading with the trend, you stand a higher chance of getting it right at the end of the day.

However, the Intraday Momentum Index is not suitable for long-term traders but for intraday traders. So long term traders will have to look for another indicator for their trade to take a suitable position.

Money Flow Index MFI

For traders looking for an indicator to predict the movements in the market for longer-term trade, the money flow index is the perfect indicator. It is suitable for stock-based trade than index base trade, so it can be used to predict the direction of the market using price and volume. The main difference between the money flow index and the relative strength index is the use of volume in the MFI and thus regarded as the weighted RSI.

This indicator measures the pressure of the trade by taking into account the inflow and outflow of money over a 14 days period. The 14 days period is the default setting of the indicator, and one can change the number of days to suit their method of trading option. The tweaking of the number of days can be used by experienced traders to gather more insight into the assets. However, the default system is fine and can be used to get the desired result, especially for newbies.

The money flow index is easy to use as it predicts the oversold and overbought region, just like most momentum indicators. MFI also alert us about a directional change of the trend, ensuring we catch the formation of a new trend early enough to take advantage of the move as it begins to form.

When the money flow index reads 80, then it is regarded that the assets are overbought, and we should not take a position to buy the assets but look for opportunities to sell or take a put option in this case. In the reverse position, when the indicator reads 20, the asset is oversold, and at this point, we are looking at the asset to make a new move and start a new trend.

The indicators give a more detailed move of the market because of the added price data than the Relative Strength Index. And it provides a clear picture for long-term traders to make an investment on their favorite asserts. It can also be used by short term traders giving a clear picture of what the price is doing over a period of days, giving you a clear picture of demand and supply in the market.

The Put-Call Ratio PRC

The put-call ratio is a market sentiment indicator, telling us between buyers and sellers, who have the upper hand in the market. With this sentiment indicator, you can know which of the side has momentum and take advantage of that drive to put yourself in a suitable position on the market.

Indicators like the pull call rational do not tell us the entry point; they only give us an insight of what is playing out in the market. It tells us if the asset is bearish and bullish, and in most cases, it is traded along with other indicators.

The pull call ratio is calculated by the put option over the call option, and the result will give us an indication of the momentum of the market. When the ratio is above 1, then the pull option is greater, and the market is bearish. On the other hand, when the ratio is less than 1, then the market is bullish as the call options are more than the pull option.

It is a simple indicator and can be understood, giving a clear indication of what the market is up to at the moment.

Open Interest OI

Open Interest, popularly known as OI, determines the strength of an existing trend and tells us if it is right to jump in or to wait for the formation of a new trend. The indicator tells us the number of open and unsettled positions in the market, which is an indicator of what buyers are doing in the market.

When there is an increase in the open interest, the trend is strong and sustainable, unlike when there is a decrease in open interest. When there is declining open interest, the trend is weakening, and it is a good time to stay away from the market and wait for the new trend. It is not advisable to use this indicator alone as you must rely on other indicators or fundamental analysis along with this indicator.

Stochastic Indicator

The stochastic indicator is another popular indicator, and this indicator can give us an indication of when to enter the market as well as the momentum of the market. It is similar to the relative strength index but has two moving average moving on the indicator. The indicator can tell us when the momentum if a trend is coming to an end.

When the price is reading above 80, then the market is at the overbought level, and we look for a selling opportunity. In the reverse case, when the price is below 20, then we are at an oversold zone and except a reversal to occur in the market. It is just like the relative strength index, eight? Yes, but we have two lines moving with the stochastic indicator, which provides us with more information on the price and volume on the market.

You can take out a pull option or call option with this indicator alone, especially when the lines cross in the indicator. One method of using this indicator to take a position in the market is when the lines cross when they are in an oversaturated zone.

When the indicator is above 80, you can look for opportunities to short the position and take a put option when there is a cross of both lines. The cross of the moving average will indicate that a new trend is forming and that this trend will be stronger. In the reverse case, when the stochastic is below 20, the buying option is saturated and in an oversold zone. At this stage, when the stochastic crosses at the zone, we will be expected a strong bullish trend to begin, and we should take a call option based on this reaction of price in the market.

The stochastic is a very important indicator for options traders as it provides us with a detailed option to trade.

There are over a hundred technical indicators that can be used for options trading; however, the indicators listed above are what we use to determine the sentiment and momentum. Using any of these technical indicators is mainly up to the traders. You should use an indicator you are comfortable with and use to form different styles and strategies for your trading.

Some indicators, as we have shown, may not be suitable for intraday trading, while others may be more efficient for intraday trading.

We just enlighten you on how technical indicators can be used to determine the market, giving you a sight of what is happening with the assets. You can use this information to plan and excite your trade as you take advantage of the information you get.

The Advantage of Technical Analyze

The debate on whether technical analysis surpassed fundamental analysis has been an old argument since the time we knew financial trade started. The answer is difficult to give directly as everyone with their different methods and strategies can implement any of their style of trading.

While technical analysis involves the use of statistics to predict the movement in the market, the fundamental analysis uses information, news, and events to determine the movement in the market. We have studied the advantage of fundamental analysis to option trade; now, we are going into details to view the advantage of technical analyses.

1. Technical analyses focus on the current price.

With fundamental analysis, you are concerned about what is happening in the world and try to input that into the chart. When using financial analysis, you do not mind what the chart is playing out at the moment but focus on what the impact of the news will have on the chart.

With attention focused on the news, you are not focused on the chart, and you may miss the move because of the time it takes you to analyze the impact of the news on the market. While technical analyses focus on what is happening in the market with prices reflecting on what the indicators are telling us.

Professional technical traders will always tell you that the technical indicators always take into account what buyers are doing on the market regardless of any other cause of market movement. I prefer trading with indicators, or if I am looking at the financial news, I prefer to have an indicator on my chart to guide me in the proper direction of the big move.

Fundamental analysis does not prepare you for a move in the market, and even when that move comes, you may miss it because it will come so fast because of the high impact. Most of the time, the information about the moves in the market is already represented in the indicator, just waiting for the news to take its impact. You will not miss the move because the indicator got you prepared to take the trade.

If you have watched how indicator reacts to preceding news that is coming up, you will see the market in a range. At this point, the indicators are also telling us that the market is thin, and they are few buyers and sellers with the market having no predominant direction. So in essence, the market is preparing us for a big move, which will come with the news.

So we might not be missing much when we focus on the technical part of the market as everything that happens takes shape with the technical indicators. And such indicators will give us a true picture of the market, although they might be some rare occasion when we see moves going against the indicator, and this also happens with fundamental indicators.

With this point, one can trade confidently with the technical indicators without giving much regard to the fundamental analysis.

2. With technical indicators, you can take advantage of the trend

To increase the probability of making money with option derivatives, it will be better if you are going with the trend. When you place trade towards the trend, the chances the market price will be way above the strike price at the expiration of the contract is high. With this, you are sure that you will make a profit for your trade than when you go against the trend.

And technical indicators help us to determine the trend of the assets and place you in a better position to go with the direction of the trend. Most of the indicators, especially those will discuss in this book, are momentum indicators. They tell us the direction of the predominating trend and if it is still active, either in an overbought or oversold zone.

These indicators give us the right direction to follow, and in most cases, they tell us when a new trend is being formed and the end of the predominating trend. When the indicator signals the end of the trend, that is when it is at the drone of overbought or oversold, and then we might be expecting the formation of a new trend or a drawback and the continuation of the predominating trend. In such a case, we will be waiting for the information of us h move and be ready to take a ride in the right direction.

When you follow the trend, especially when you catch the trend at its early formation, you are going to make a huge profit in that trade. The market price will be distant from the strike price, which will land you in profit at the expiration of the contract.

The indicators also let us know when to stay out of the market and wait for the best time to enter. Technical indicators interpret when the market is at the range when investors are skeptical and are away from the market, waiting for the right opportunity to come in the market. At this stage, the market is not making any move, and it will be risky to take a trade at this stage. So the technical indicators also help us to stay away from the market when it is too tight and unpredictable. It will not only tell us where to trade but when not to trade.

3. Predict the duration of the trend

We have ascertained the importance of the trend and why it is important to stay with the trend. Another challenge trader will face determining how long the trend lasts.

This is easy to achieve with the indicator and the time frame we are using to take the trade. While some indicators are designed specifically to tell us the direction of the intraday trend, others are suitable for telling us the overall or long-term trend in the market and if we can stay with that trade for more than a day. The intraday trend is for that day, usually short-term position on the trade while the long-term indicators we will take long term trade on them.

Also, we can determine the length of the trade with the time frame we are using, such as 1 hour, 4 hours, daily, weekly, and monthly. With this time frame, we can determine the expiration date of the assets just like 1 hour, 15 minutes is all intraday time frame. The 4 hours' time frame and higher time frames are for long-term trade that may last more than a day and up to a month for swing traders.

While the fundamental analysis cannot help us with the period the effect of the news will last, technical analyses will be helpful in that aspect. And this is a good reason to use technical analysis over fundamental analysis to make reasonable and flexible decisions in your trade.

4. Technical analysts are based on history.

Are you popular with the phrase, history repeats itself?

That is how technical analysis programmed to work, and we expect made patterns to form and repeat the same behavior as the previous day. Technical analysts are based on historical behavior of the financial market to events happening now in the marker.

The prices react in the chart forming different patterns based on buyers' and sellers' emotions. These patterns are repetitive as investors face the same situation with the market and react with the sand emotions to what is happening in the market. You would remember that we mentioned backtesting on the previous chart to watch how they reacted to certain circumstances in the market; it is believed that if those similar circumstances repeat it, the market will behave in the same matter, and that is due to technical analyses observed on the chart.

You should understand that the pattern may not be a complete mirror image of what happened earlier, but it will look similar. But we should have an understanding of what to expect with these technical analyze and prepare to take the corresponding action on the platform.

We have many traders watching that same technical set up and are waiting for the right set up to take place. They will enter the trade as soon as the setup is confirmed, which will increase the volume of the trade in that direction and sent the trade riding with speed and momentum because of the volume of traders taking that trade.

This is one of the reasons why popular technical indicators like the relative strength index are popular with traders as a huge number of technical traders are studying the indicator. And another reason why some other popular indicators are built based on the relative strength index and added some little parameters to make it easier to enter the trade with the supportive indicator. So use technical indicators for backtesting any of your strategies to gauge their winning rate before you jump into using the strategy. This is the perfect way to learn options trading before you jump into the market as you can gather experience with backtesting of the asset and improve your trading skills before you get into the market.

I have come across many strategies, and backtesting is one of the methods I used in selecting the strategy I am using. With several strategies at my disposal, I have to place each on a chart and backtest them over several months back to check out the consistency both in prices and volume of the methods. I finally settle for the one I am using based on the high rate of successful trade and the frequency of trades I get per week using this particular strategy. It was also easy for me and complimented my style of trade.

So backtesting will give us an edge in planning and selecting the best indicators that will suit our personal style. If you are an intraday trader, you can backtest your strategies using the indicators based on the intraday time frame, such as 1 hour and below. For long-term traders, they will want to backtest their strategies on 4 hours and above timeframe to check out how long the trends likely to last with these strategies.

On the other hand, with fundamental analysis, it is difficult to analyze how history works because the information and the pattern of reaction are not captured on the chart.

5. Time to enter the trade

With fundamental analysis, you may not know when the move may occur, or the news may occur so fast that you may not have the time to get in and take advantage of the move. Technical analyses will prepare you when the market is about to make a huge move, and you will be available to take that huge move.

When we see the market on a range with indicators, experienced traders know it is only a matter of time before the range break out, and we will experience a high move. Since the technical indicators can predict the momentum, like you, when the market is oversold or overbought, we can have a high probability of predicting the direction the huge move direction will be and prepare to follow that trend.

Fundamental analyses, we might be expecting high impact news, but no likely knowledge of where it will go until the market starts reacting to the news. It may be too late to enter and make money from the market with such erratic and unpredictable behavior.

With the timing of when to get the best out of the market, we will be watching the indicator for when they give us a signal that the big move is about to take place.

6. Technical indicators work on any timeframe

Technical indicators can be applied to any timeframe, and you will get your suitable result at any time you choose. Indicators follow a regular pattern, and this does not change with the time frame you are using. Any time frame will give you the same pattern, and you can trade successfully on the chosen time frame.

With fundamental analyses and when trading high impact news, the noise in some of the time frames, especially the shorter time like 1 hour and 15 minutes, may not give you an ideal picture of what is happening. So with trading news, you have to move to the bigger time frame for a clear picture of what is going on in the market. So it is difficult for short-term traders to trade with the news for the moves mat be too erratic for the intraday traders to make any useful impact.

The pattern formed on indicators is the same with any time frame, so the strategy you learn with an indicator can be applied on any timeframe and suit your style of trading. The inconsistencies of fundamentals with timeframes and style of trading are one of the reasons why most traders stay away from high impact news.

7. Technical Analysis works on all market

It does not matter the market you are trying using technical analysis; the result is the same, and you can apply it to other financial instruments. It is like it is universal, and you can get anyone to teach you using any of the financial instruments.

Like when I started trading, I did not learn technical analysis with trading options. I learn using indicators with Forex, and it was a profitable venture. I have tried shares and options derivatives using this technical knowledge, and it works well. So technical analysis has a wider approach, and you can use it in the future in any of the financial markets.

The disadvantage of Technical Analyses

Everything has its advantages and disadvantages and so does technical analysis, while it is very good, it also has its downside.

Some of the cons of using technical analyses include:

1. It can be confusing, selecting from a wide range of technical indicators. These may leave traders confused, especially when they have learned a lot of technical indicators and want to put them to test.

2. Technical indicators may be misleading at times, especially when they are used without support or knowledge of the chart.

3. It may leave your chart all clogged up and difficult to understand.

Understanding both types of analyses can be of huge benefit to traders as they can combine both effectively for a better result. To be honest, you cannot trade without a little understanding of technical analyses as the chart reading requires technical knowledge.

The technical analyses not only give you direction for your trade, but they also provide you with the target. And I guess no trader can trade successfully without knowledge of technical analyses.

Chapter 7

Options Trading Strategy

There are several strategies you can find trading options, and you can also develop your personal strategies based on what you are familiar with what we have studied.

I am sure by now; you may have tried some ways of predicting the marketing using some of the fundamental and technical analyses we have discussed above. But don't worry, we have some tested strategies we will share with you to help you trade successfully.

However, before you start trading, you have to understand some terms that will save you a lot in this business, and they include:

1. Risk Management: you should know how much you are willing to risk on a trade and avoid blowing your account on just a few trades.

2. Purpose of trading options: to give yourself purpose in the market and stay focus, always have an idea of why you are reading options. Is it for profit, hedging funds, or long-term investment?

3. What's your strategy? : Find a suitable strategy that suits your personality and sticks with that strategy. Changing strategies will make you unstable, and you may end up blowing your account.

4. Manage losses: the problem with some traders is that they cannot manage losses. They become agitated when they lose and began to make irrational moves

5. Plan your trade: draw a plan and stick with that plan to stay successful. Read the plan each day until it becomes a part of you.

Now we are going to look at some of the strategies we have selected for our readers so they can make an impact in the market.

But before we jump into the strategies, we should have a clear understanding of the word option and how it works. Most traders use options for making money, and few use it for hedging funds or something minor purpose. And if you must make money on options, you have to understand what you are doing and what you should do. Options trading is becoming popular, and many people have not really gotten the whole idea behind option trade.

For one, you do not necessarily need to hold a position until it expires to make money. You can sell off a put or call position at any time to either make money or cut your losses. This is one of the reasons most people fail with options; they lack the knowledge of what to do.

You can sell off a contract when you are at a profit but believe that the market may change and may start reading negative soon.

All of this may come from the analysis you have read from the fundamental or technical analysis. Also, your contract may be negative, and the best thing now is to sell off the contract to manage your lose. So you should be able to analyze these into the strategy you are using and make an effective decision

Covered Call Writing CCW

The Covered Call Writing is one of the simplest strategies you can come across, and it is a very profitable no matter how the market ends in the expiration date. I will recommend this strategy for any newbie, and it is simple to execute, and you have nothing to lose and much to gain in the market once it is executed.

For a covered call writing, you will be selling or writing off your options or shares as the case may be to another trader. In this type of trader, you will set the sale of your option and the expiration date, and you should understand that this is an option you own. You own the option, and you are willing to pass the ownership to another trader.

You set the strike price that you want the option to be sold along with the expiration date, and when it is exercised, you keep your cash premium. Remember that you are selling shares or options in 100s, and keeping your cash premium is the first gain you make with these strategies even though the option is still active.

As soon as you set the contract to sell your option, the cash premium is deposited in your account regardless if the contract was exercised or not, the cash premium is yours. If the contract expires without being exercised, your cash premium is intact as the contract becomes worthless, but you can always set to sell the contract again.

If the contract is exercised, you will sell it at an agreed price when the strike price is reached, and you lose control of that option. Your cash will be transferred to your account, and you have gained the premium plus the cash you used in selling the contract.

You can see that it is a straightforward strategy, and no matter what happens, you have to gain on the trade. You can try out this strategy or learn more about it online.

Naked Put

A naked put is another options trading strategy that involves the selling of a stock option that is out of money OTM. In this instance, the stock price is higher than the strike price, and you out this contract for sale as you collect your cash premium in hand.

Note that you stand the chance of buying the option when the stock price is lower than the strike price, and the option is in profit. Also, on the expiration of the contract, the cash premium is your reward, and you might still have the opportunity or pitting the contract up for sale.

One reason I like this strategy is that you are left better off if the market does not go in your favor at the end as you will have collected your cash premium, and you may also collect the settlement once a buyer exercises the contract so you would have gained from the transaction.

The Credit Spread Method

This is a cautious method suitable for beginners as they learn the role of options trading and maintain a suitable balance in their account. The method reduces the probability of loss by selling off a portion of your contract while buying another portion instead of throwing all of it up for sale.

Credits spread method is regarded by some traders as being too cautious, especially since you will miss out on making a big profit if the market goes your way. Yes, that is true, but nothing is certain on the financial market, and most experienced traders will tell you that the best way to stay in Forex is to minimize your losses while adding up your profit gradually.

With the credit-spread method, you may encounter many losses before your account finally dries out, and that is why it is recommended for beginners. My first few years of trading saw me blow up several accounts because of over-trading and risking too much in trades. I focus more on what the profit to make in the trade than considering the risk I am being exposed to, and in a few months, the losses begin to pile up exponentially till the accounts ran out dry.

Thus, good money management and a strategy that helps you in minimizing your loss are vital for newbie as they learn what it is like trading options in real life. This method is also suitable for those that are patient in building up their account steadily and in no haste to make money. Remember that the market is always there, no matter if you lose or gain, and there is always more money to make.

So these are some of the strategies that you can use in options trading, especially for a newbie. They are as simple as they sound, but getting to the market can be a different ball game.

Remember to check what is happening in the market as you hold or intend to sell your option. The market changes due to different factors, and since you may not be aware of the factors that are affecting the market, it will be best if you keep an eye on the market by checking the appropriate chants.

They are other strategies out there, but these ones are much simpler and easier to trade than other complicated ones. You can also come up with your own strategy to play within the market and make money.

Chapter 8

Trading Psychology

Now in trading, you have to possess the right mindset to succeed as a trader. Many traders jump into the market without knowing the essence of trading, and all they think about is how to make money.

We understand that the main reason why most people trade is to make money, but this should not be the first thing on our mind when setting out on this business. Starting up options trading like other financial markets will require that you have the right mindset in executing your trade, watching your trade, taking your profit. One of the main reasons traders' losses in financial markets is their attitude.

So in this chapter, we are going to analyze how our attitudes can make us succeed in options trading. After you are through with this chapter, you are going to feel that all you need is the right attitude and approach to trading the financial markets.

We are going to discuss some of these factors and how they will help you become a good trader. This chapter will focus on the human aspect of being a good trader and the qualities you have to develop to succeed as an options trader.

Being Patient

Patience is required in the beginning to become a good trader. In learning how to trade, you have to be patient in learning the tricks and tips involved in trading. Trading is a complex process that involves daily routine that you have to follow with your trade plan. To keep up with this routine, you have to be patient with the process.

The first phase of options trading is learning how to trade and all the requirements you will need to know about the option. Reading this book is part of the process of learning how to trade options, and you have been patient to this point. You should continue with being patient in trading as many traders have lost their investment in an attempt to try and go ahead of the market.

You must have a strategy in trading options after you have carried out proper research and come up with one that suits your style. Being patient with your strategy is key to becoming a successful trader as you see your plan to the end and take your profit or loss.

A lot of traders have become wishful in their trader as they abandon their plan to try and take a quick one to make a profit. In the long run, the trade may go against them when they fail to follow their strategy. Whenever you find yourself being controlled by the will to force the market, without a clear signal from your plan, close the computer and walk away, so you do not make unnecessarily trade.

Wishful thinking will never make your account grow, as you cannot wish the market to make your bid. Do your best to stick to your plan and continuously follow that plan until it becomes a habit.

Start Small

The financial market is not going anywhere since it has been around before you started trading, and it will be around if you lose your capital today. So do not be in haste to make money with options trade as you will have enough time to make money as you start slow.

When opening your first account, search for a broker that offers the minimal deposit and register with that broker. Start with the minimal amount required by the broker and watch how you increase your capital with that broker. The reason you should start with a small capital and grow it gradually is to teach you money management and patience in trading with options.

Starting small will remove the pressure of trying to increase your account quickly, so you are more relaxed taking each trade as they come. Too many traders have lost their investment going in with everything they have too fast, so do not make similar mistakes. Reading and practicing with backtesting and the demo account is different from playing the game with real money, so use as little capital as possible to get the real feeling of it before you put in your savings into the market.

The market is not going anywhere; it will be there next week for you to make money, so there is no point being in haste. Watch how you perform with the small investment, and then gradually watch the performance of your account before you invest big in the market.

Good Money Management

The more you invest in a trade, the more you profit and also the higher the risk of your capital as you can also lose sustain amount in the trade. You might have $500 in your account and risk $100 on a trade, and in the end, you might gain double that and increase your capital. That would have been a good bargain, but imagine if the trade had gone against you, then you would have lost more than 25% of your capital.

This is a huge risk when you consider how much you are going to lose, and if you lose five trades with the same risk, then you would have blown off the account. Such a terrible money management strategy is too risky, and traders make the mistake of viewing the price they will gain rather than the risk they are taking.

A wise trader will put risk management upfront as the key point in every single trade you will make to safeguard the funds. Imagine risking $50 or less on each trade with a $500 account; you would have had more trades to lose to wipe out completely. And I am sure you are not going to lose five trades without a win if you follow your plans and stick to your objectives as you gradually increase your capital.

I am sure if you are consistent with good money management, you will grow your account over a certain period of time. If you have been consistent in making a profit, growing your account, then you will be ready to move on to a bigger account. You may move to a more prominent broker who offers extensive services for experience trader as you bring in your expertise to play at this stage.

Trading is a gradual process, it is not a get rich quick scheme, and you will become profitable in the long run if you stick to your process.

Selecting a Strategy

The strategy is an important aspect if you want to succeed in options trading, as you cannot make options out of the blue. Developing your own strategy will require some years of experience in the market; as a newbie, you will have to rely on strategies like the ones discussed in this book.

For beginners, you can use any of the easy strategies, and as you gain experience, you can develop your own strategies. Developing a strategy will require you to understand how to use fundamental and technical analyses to read and predict the market. One other way traders have found to trade options easily is to buy signals or use programs that can predict the market.

Although there is no guarantee with these signals, some people, especially those too busy to follow the market, another way the trader uses to follow the market is to follow signals delivered by more successful traders as you copy them and do the same. All these are easy ways to trade the market, but it is better to learn how to do it on your own.

Even if you are not going to trade on your own as you may decide to use an expert trader's advice or using a program to predict trades for you, it is better if you have an idea of what is going on in the market.

Take a Break from a Bad Day

You do not have to trade every day, especially when you are having a bad day, when you make three consistent bad trade, go off from your computer and do something else. At times being on the computer, especially when you do not find a good signal, can be frustrating, and instead of staying online, you might decide to do something else, so you are not forced into taking a position.

Frustration can make a trader enter a position when there is no signal based on the strategy they are using. And they enter the trade based on wishful thinking and begin to wish the market goes their way. To be honest, wishing thinking will hardly move the market in the direction you place your trade. More than half of the time traders take a position based on wishes, without following their strategy, the market usually goes against them, and they lose their trade.

When you are feeling the frustration creeping in, just walk away from the computer or take a day away from trading. Don't let frustration lead you to take a position without following through your plan and avoid any wishful trading. If you have been trading for a while, you may have come across some days when everything keeps going bad right from the first day. Any trade you take that day may end up going bad and no matter what you do nothing will seem to go right, so when a day begins like that, stay away from the market, tomorrow is another day, and the money will still be there to make in the market.

Choose a timeframe that Suits Your Style

I don't get how people can trade using multiple timeframes; it can really mess up my trade plan as the other timeframe will cause confusion. One key to being successful in trading is to select a suitable time frame that will suit your style and your availability. Some people cannot trade intraday because their schedule will not allow the trader to follow the intraday time frame, so they may end up becoming a swing trader.

If you want to play the intraday game and your schedule will not allow you to focus on the necessary timeframe like the 1-hour timeframe and below, then you will face difficulties. You may end up missing out on opportunities and may be forced to trade whenever you have a chance to look at the chart. This will make you take some calls that do not correspond with your signal, which may affect your trade.

In such a case, you will have to play your trade to fit into your schedule so you can benefit from the market easily. If you are busy all through the day, you can opt for the 4-hour timeframe and above, and you will find time to check updates and make reasonable calls and put decisions for the option derivatives.

Plan your trade along with your regular schedule and choose a timeframe that suits your routine so you will have the time to check for opportunities when they present themselves with the appropriate chart. You will not miss opportunities when you are using the right time frame for your plan.

How do you handle your loss?

The way traders handle losses in the market is important for the psychology of the trader and how they will perform in the market. Some traders react to losses very badly, and with each loss, they are seeking to change their strategies, feeling that their plan has failed them.

No trading plan is 100% fail-proof, and if you can get a 70% success rate, then you are in a good place. There are times when the plan will fail you, but that does not mean that you will change the plan. When you lose, do not go on a revenge trade and try to gain back what you lost instantly. Accept the loss and move on while you stick to your plan and wait for the next set up to present itself before you take the next move.

Losses are inevitable in the financial market, and you must take them when they come and do not allow the losses to destabilize you.

Because losses are inevitable, you have to employ a good money management strategy, so you don't dent your capital with some of the few losses.

Keep it Simple

You do not need complex strategies or analyses to trade options as the simplest strategies can do the trick. Building strategies with too many technical indicators can become confusing as the indicators might end up giving different readings and signals in the market. This can create conflicting signals that may affect your trade.

In the financial market, the trick is to keep it simple and repeat whatever you are doing. While trading for the first time, I was into technical analysis, and on my charts, I may have not less than three indicators on the chart. It was chaotic and confusing that I do not know which one to focus on, and this causes me some opportunities.

Not until I resolved to a single indicator, which was my favorite amongst the entire indicator that I began to experience some sanity and success in my trade. I found out that keeping it simple was less stressful and profitable as they were less confusion with a clean chart to focus on.

Trading psychology is important for you to get the right mindset when trading the financial markets. There is a course on the financial market that dwells on trading psychology and the mindset that is involved in trading the financial market, and this shows the importance of the mindset.

The right attitude can make a successful or a bad trader, and the wrong attitude can ruin your account no matter the foolproof strategies you employ in the market. While developing your plans and strategies, ensure to develop the right attitude and find ways to maintain them in your lifestyle.

Conclusion

Options trading is different from other forms of financial markets, but if you have experience trading shares, stock, Forex, and other forms of trading, it will be of help. You can use the experience of other forms of financial instruments to predict the market so it will be easier for those with these experiences.

However, inexperienced traders can also trade options, as we have learned in this book. This book would have brought more insight for you as you prepare to get into the market with the basic knowledge we provided. We were able to introduce the concept of option trading in the book and how it differs from other financial instruments. Although they are slight differences, the concept of trading these instruments is similar and can be employed to one another. So it is easier for someone with experience trading other instruments for trading options successfully.

However, the newbie with little or no experience in the financial market can pick up easily and start trading as soon as possible. They just need to pick up with the basics of options trading, the basic terminology, and learn how to place orders with options. We should remember that the option is a time base contract, and our profit or loss is registered at the end of the contract. However, we still sell the contract before it expires to minimize our loss or make a profit in the market.

One area I would like the inexperienced traders to focus on is the process of taking orders in the market; they have to spend time learning the basic terminologies and what they stand for and how to use these terms. They have to grasp the use of technical and fundamental indicators to open options and follow up on the trades so they can minimize their losses and make a profit. If you have traded Forex or shares, then these analyses will be convenient for you, and options will be easier for you as you get familiar with the terms. But the newbie will have to take deep courses in reading charts with fundamental and technical analyses.

We also discussed the brokers, and we provided you with options for some selected broker. And it does not matter what kind of trader you are; you can choose from any of the brokers provided as you find one that suits your style. The brokers you use are very important in helping you to become a good trader. There are brokers who will provide help to newbie's and make them become a decent trader, while some are more focused on experienced traders. In summary, you should select the broker that meets up with the requirement as a trader to be able to grow and become a better trader.

Trading options can give you higher returns than other forms of financial instruments. And that is why more people are getting interested in trading options. But you will require the right knowledge to be able to trade it successfully. A good strategy and patience are required in the market, and this has seen many people fail and lost several accounts on trading options. Do not make the mistake of viewing options as a bet, where you can put your money on any position without proper analyzes on the market.

Option trading goes beyond learning the strategies, taking profits, and maintaining losses. The book also teaches how you can get it right and make a profit with the perfect attitude.

Trading psychology has become popular over the years as it is believed the way we behave and react to news determine our success in the market. So we need to get it right, not only with our attitude towards trading but also with our mindset.

Making money is a continuous process, and one has to be consistent with what you are doing. And our main aim as a trader is to make money continuously. Although no plan can guarantee you 100% with financial trading but with consistency, you can actually grow your account.

There are people making a living out of options trading, and this is due to the consistency in their trade. It is not that they do not register losses, but their success rate is more than their losses, and they have a good money management system.

A good management system should not have your account depleted in half after just a few losses. When you have a good management system, losses will not get you upset at the market; rather, you will pick up easily because you know your account cannot be affected by that loss. But when you have bad management, any loss will have a huge impact on your account, and a few losses will ruin your account.

It takes time to become profitable in trading, and your first few months may not go as you will expect. The process of trading is a continuous learning process, and you have to research all the time to improve your trading. It will do you a great deal if you have a mentor, someone you can look up to, especially when there consistent bad days in the market.

A mentor will encourage you and give you the zeal to continue with your quest. I will advise you not to view trading as a means of making money. Take it as a science or art of learning the market, and this will give you a different view of trading. When entering the market each day, do not think of how much you are going to make, but on how many trades you are going to get right.

You should view the market from successful trade and not making money. With good management of your account, 7 out of 10 successful trade will put you in a good place of making money. And that should be our aim in options trading, to get a high proportion of successful trade to losses.

In the market, you have to know what when to hold an asset and when to let them go. When you let go of an asset either in profit or in loss, you will be managing the profit as well as minimizing your loss. Do not compound loss, and if your readings tell you the market is not getting better, and then cut your losses.

The same goes for when you are in a profit, by taking an analysis of the market, you can determine that the market or trend is coming to an end and take your profit.

In trading, you are going to find yourself in the process and choose what is good for you. Take your time to get the feel of trading, and it will come to you. With trading, you will discover yourself as you learn more about discipline and other personal attributes that will affect your lifestyle.

As you have decided to read this book and learn about options trading, we wish you the best as you take in the practical as well as fundamental aspects of this book and apply them to yourself. You will be on your way to becoming a successful trader.

Manufactured by Amazon.ca
Bolton, ON